The old lighthouse at Withernsea, East Yorkshire. The tapering white octagonal tower was built in 1892–3 by Trinity House and was in use until June 1976; it is now in the care of Withernsea Lighthouse Museum Trust. The walls of the brick and concrete tower are 5 feet (1.5 metres) thick, and its height is 120 feet (37 metres). The light was converted to electricity in 1936, giving it a maximum range of 17 miles (27 km).

Lighthouses

Lynn F. Pearson

Published in 2008 by Shire Publications Ltd,
Midland House, West Way, Botley, Oxford OX2 0PH, UK.
(Website: www.shirebooks.co.uk)

British Library Cataloguing in Publication Data:
Pearson, Lynn F.
Lighthouses. – 2nd ed. – (Shire album; 312)
1. Lighthouses – Great Britain – History
I. Title
378.1'55'0941
ISBN-13: 978 0 7478 0556 4

Front cover: *Roker Pier lighthouse was commissioned in 1903 and stands at the seaward end of the curving 2880 feet (878 metres) long Roker Pier in Sunderland. The grade II listed granite tower was designed by Henry Hay Wake, engineer to the River Wear Commissioners. Its original lens was replaced by sealed beam lamps in 1976, and these in turn were upgraded in 2007. The brilliant white light flashes once every five seconds and can be seen up to 22 miles (35 kilometres) away.*

ACKNOWLEDGEMENTS
The author wishes to thank Penny Beckett, Richard Ellis, Trevor Ermel of Monochrome, Harry and Margaret Fancy, Tony and Kathy Herbert, Peter Hope Jones, Joan Hague, Sue Hudson, Peter Kelly, Biddy Macfarlane, John Rotheroe, Ken Trethewey, Association of Lighthouse Keepers, Commissioners of Irish Lights, Essex County Council Planning Department, Happisburgh Lighthouse Trust, Isle of Man Victorian Society, Landmark Trust, Lighthouse Society of Great Britain, North Tyneside Borough Council, Northern Lighthouse Board, the staff of Souter Lighthouse (National Trust), Tiles and Architectural Ceramics Society, Trinity House Lighthouse Service and Withernsea Lighthouse Museum Trust for their assistance in the preparation of this book. National Grid References are used with the permission of the Controller of Her Majesty's Stationery Office.
    Photographs are acknowledged as follows: Richard Ellis, pages 10, 25 (bottom); Tony Herbert, page 57 (bottom); Peter Hope Jones, pages 13, 26; John Kirkwood, cover; Cadbury Lamb, pages 5 (bottom), 11, 12 (bottom), 14 (bottom), 22 (centre), 24 (bottom), 39 (left), 42 (both), 58; North Tyneside Borough Council, page 22 (bottom); Ken Trethewey, Lighthouse Society of Great Britain, pages 4, 21 (bottom), 24 (top), 31, 35 (centre), 36 (bottom), 53 (both). Other photographs are by the author.

Printed in Malta by Gutenberg Press Limited, Gudja Road, Tarxien PLA 19, Malta.

Contents

Private lights and public provision 4

The first rock lighthouses 11

Lighthouse construction in the nineteenth century 18

Showing the light 25

The lightkeeper and the modern lighthouse 32

A selective gazetteer of British and Irish lighthouses ... 38

Further reading 61

Websites 61

Places to visit 62

Index of lighthouses 64

The view south across the Thames to the North Greenwich peninsula and the Dome, from Bow Creek lighthouse on Trinity Buoy Wharf, Tower Hamlets, London. The lighthouse, built in 1864–6, is the only survivor of a pair of lighthouses used by Trinity House in lighting trials. Trinity Buoy Wharf is now an arts and business centre and is normally open to the public.

Private lights and public provision

The need for seamarks – towers, beacons, lighthouses and other 'landmarks' used by seafarers – is as old as the existence of maritime trading. The first lighthouses were built on the shores of the Mediterranean, perhaps during the fifth century BC, but the earliest structure for which written records exist is the lighthouse on the island of Pharos, off the harbour of Alexandria on the northern coast of Egypt. This monumental lighthouse, which was built between 283 and 247 BC, reached 466 feet (142 metres) in height, making it the tallest stone tower in the world until it collapsed during an earthquake in 1326. Such was the fame of the lighthouse that by the sixteenth century the word 'pharos' had become synonymous with lighthouse, and the study of lighthouses eventually became known as pharology.

Lighthouses were commonplace in the Mediterranean by the first century BC and appeared at major ports throughout the Roman empire. The pharos at Dover Castle, overlooking the harbour, was built by the Romans in the late first or early second century AD; it still survives, although it has been much altered.

The lighthouse or pharos that now stands within the grounds of Dover Castle, Kent, was built by the Romans in the late first or early second century AD. It is likely that the flint rubblestone tower originally had eight storeys and was faced with stone. There were no stairs linking the wooden floors, indicating that ladders must have been used to reach the top fire platform. Many alterations were made when the structure was used as a church bell-tower in medieval times.

The east and west Lawe Top Beacons, South Shields, were built in 1832 as daymarks to assist ships entering the river Tyne; seen directly in line, they indicated a safe route into the port. They replaced eighteenth-century beacons on the same site, high ground known as The Lawe, overlooking the mouth of the river. The obelisks, which cost £60, each have a stone base, brick upper part and stone cap.

In its original form it was an octagonal stone tower, reaching about 79 feet (24 metres) in height, with a top platform on which a fire burned.

Few lighthouses were erected between the end of the Roman empire and the eleventh century. The earliest medieval lights in the British Isles were established by the church. Celtic monks may have displayed a light on Hook Head, at the entrance to Waterford harbour on the south-eastern coast of Ireland, during the early twelfth century. The Hook Head lighthouse, a defended tower, was built on the same site around 1172. By the mid thirteenth century it was being maintained by Augustinian canons, who had the right to collect tolls from shipping entering the harbour. Hook is the oldest lighthouse in the British Isles still in use as a working light. Its stone tower, almost circular in cross-section, originally stood 59 feet (18 metres) high; after minor alterations in the seventeenth century, a central turret was added to the twelfth-century structure in 1864.

The lighthouse at St Catherine's, near the southern tip of the Isle of Wight, the highest point of the island, was built in the early fourteenth century and rebuilt around 1323. It was later used as an

Hook Head lighthouse, County Wexford, one of the oldest lighthouses in the world, was built around 1172 as a defended stone tower, roughly circular in cross-section, standing 59 feet (18 metres) high. The light ceased in 1641 but was re-established around 1667; a glazed, wooden lantern was added in 1687 to enclose the coal fire. Twelve Argand oil lamps with reflectors were fitted in the late 1790s by Thomas Rogers, who also erected a new lantern; this was replaced in 1864. A visitor centre was opened at the lighthouse in 2001.

Although a light was shown on North Foreland, just north of Broadstairs, Kent, as early as 1499, the first lighthouse on the site was an octagonal wooden tower built in 1636 by Sir John Meldrum. It was burned out in 1659 and its replacement was destroyed by fire in 1683. The present lighthouse, an octagonal brick and flint tower 39 feet (12 metres) high, was built in 1691. Two storeys were added to the tower in 1793, and the lighthouse was bought by Trinity House in 1832. Lightkeepers' houses were added at either side of the tower during 1840–50. North Foreland was the final Trinity House light to be automated, the last keeper leaving on 26th November 1998.

oratory (a small chapel) by local monks, but only the light tower remains, although the structure is still known as St Catherine's Oratory. The 36 feet (11 metres) high tower is a sturdy stone structure with an octagonal cross-section and four fin-like buttresses. Unlike most medieval lighthouses, where illumination was by open fire, the tower was topped by a glazed lantern that sheltered a small fire or lamp. The combination of eight small windows, each measuring only 1 foot 3 inches (0.38 metres) across, and the prevalence of fog meant the light was of little practical use to shipping.

Around thirty to forty lighthouses are known to have existed in the British Isles during the medieval period, many of them located on the south coast of England. Apart from a small number of substantial lighthouses maintained by the church, lights were generally shown from chapels and fortifications and at harbour entrances. Building and manning the light, providing ample fuel and showing a good light in all weather conditions taxed the resources and organisation of medieval townships. Funds were normally derived from tolls on passing ships, collected when they entered the nearest harbour.

By the sixteenth century the poor state of coastal lighting was giving such cause for concern that the responsibility was passed to the Corporation of Trinity House, which originated as a medieval guild of mariners. Its early history is unknown, but its main concern appears to have been the welfare of ex-seamen and their families. In 1513 a group of London mariners, with great expertise in navigation along the Thames, petitioned Henry VIII to re-form the mariners' guild, partly in order to retain their near-monopoly on local navigation. They were granted a royal charter in 1514, the guild becoming known as the Brotherhood of Trinity House and Deptford Strond. Similar brotherhoods existed at Hull and Newcastle upon Tyne; the charter granted to the latter in 1536 marks the first association between Trinity House and

Right: *A plaque on the exterior of the banqueting hall built in 1721 for Trinity House of Newcastle upon Tyne; this private corporation had responsibility for lighthouses from 1536, although building began on its quayside site in 1505. Almshouses, a chapel and a rigging loft were also part of the Trinity House courtyard complex.*

Below: *Lowestoft was the site of the first lighthouses to be built by Trinity House, a pair of leading lights, in 1609. They were rebuilt in 1628 and in 1676, when the rear light was moved up on to the cliff. Constant changes in the approach to Lowestoft resulted in the rebuilding of the low light in 1730 and again in 1832, the latter structure being designed by Richard Suter, a pupil of Daniel Asher Alexander. In 1867 James Douglass replaced the low light with a wrought-iron structure that could be easily re-sited; it was moved inland in 1894, but discontinued in 1923. The present lighthouse, a 52 feet (16 metres) high white tower rising above keepers' cottages on the cliff top, was built in 1874.*

Below: *The old lighthouse on Flamborough Head, to the east of Bridlington, was built by the entrepreneur Sir John Clayton in 1674. However, the toll on passing ships was inadequate to fund the lighthouse, which was never lit. The octagonal chalk rubblestone tower is about 79 feet (24 metres) high with four floors. The design economically combined the function of lighthouse and dwelling for the lightkeeper.*

lighthouses, as it licensed the brethren to build two light towers at North Shields.

An Act of Parliament of 1566 allowed the Corporation of Trinity House to erect lights on the coast of England and Wales, at its own cost. However, it was 1609 before the Corporation's first lighthouse was erected, at Lowestoft on the Suffolk coast, and as Trinity House had not been granted a monopoly this slow beginning encouraged private entrepreneurs to consider building lights as a profit-making exercise. Private lighthouse ownership became popular, particularly during the late seventeenth century.

John Meldrum, an ex-soldier, gained the right to build lighthouses at the North and South Forelands, Kent, and Orfordness, Suffolk, in 1635. All three were profitable ventures, as were the

Between 1770 and 1806, 174 ships perished off Flamborough Head. The present Flamborough lighthouse was built by Trinity House in 1806; the round, white tower was designed by the architect Samuel Wyatt, consultant engineer to the Corporation, with construction by John Matson of Bridlington. The elegant white-painted brick tower, which was increased in height to 89 feet (27 metres) in 1925, contains only the spiral stone stair; the lightkeepers lived in adjoining cottages.

Harwich leading lights erected by Sir William Batten, Surveyor of the Navy, in 1665. Less fortunate was Sir John Clayton, a gentleman and something of an innovator, who built five lighthouses during the 1660s and 1670s, at Flamborough Head, the Farne Islands, Cromer and Corton (near Lowestoft), where two were erected. Only two of Sir John's towers – the pair at Corton – were ever lit, as the dues turned out to be insufficient. In Ireland Sir Robert Reading built five lighthouses during the 1660s, on the eastern and southern coasts.

Private lights flourished in England until the early nineteenth century, when increasing complaints from seafarers concerning high tolls resulted in Parliament setting up a select committee in 1834 to investigate lighthouse administration. An Act of Parliament was passed in 1836, abolishing private lights in England and Wales, and providing funds for the purchase of private lights by Trinity House. The last lighthouse to remain in private hands was the Skerries, off the north-west coast of Anglesey and near the shipping route to the port of Liverpool. In

The first lighthouse on Lizard Point, the most southerly point of mainland Britain, was built in 1619, but the light ceased within around ten years. Twin lighthouses were then erected in 1752, both octagonal towers; this double light distinguished Lizard from St Agnes, in the Isles of Scilly. The towers were rebuilt in 1812 by Trinity House, and eventually the double light was reduced to a single on the easterly tower; a new lantern was fitted around 1904.

There was a light on Spurn Head as early as 1427. High and low lights were built in 1674, then two new lighthouses were built by John Smeaton for Trinity House in 1771–6. The high light was 90 feet (27 metres) high and the low light 50 feet (15 metres); both were brick towers. Apart from Eddystone, these two towers were the only lighthouses to be built by Smeaton, who pursued a wide-ranging engineering career. The low light, shown here, was rebuilt in 1852 but went out of service when a new high light was lit in 1895. The low light is now topped by a water tank, which supplied the keepers' cottages, while the old high light was demolished in 1895.

1841, after years of negotiation, Trinity House paid its owners the huge sum of £444,984 for this lucrative light. The Corporation has had full responsibility for the lighthouses of England, Wales, Gibraltar and the Channel Islands, apart from some harbour lights, since 1836.

Its best-known engineers came from the Douglass family. Nicholas Douglass worked for Trinity House from 1839, supervising construction of the first and second Bishop Rock lights, off Land's End. His son James Nicholas Douglass was

Dunnet Head is the most northerly lighthouse in mainland Britain. It was built by Robert Stevenson in 1830–3; building materials were brought by boat from Brough, just over 2 miles (3 km) away at the base of the headland. Landings were made on the stone jetty in the inlet at Brough, where a store used during construction of the lighthouse still stands.

Rinrawros Point or Aranmore lighthouse stands on the north-western tip of Aran Island, off Dunglow in Donegal. The first lighthouse on the site, a granite tower, was built in 1798 by Thomas Rogers, and the second, a 233 feet (71 metres) high tower, was erected on the ruins of the first in 1865.

Engineer-in-Chief to Trinity House during 1863–92 and was responsible for around twenty new lights, including the fourth Eddystone, off Plymouth. William Douglass, brother of James Nicholas, worked for Trinity House before moving to Ireland, where he built eight new lights between 1878 and 1898.

Lighthouse administration in Scotland was reorganised in 1786, with the establishment of the Commissioners of Northern Lighthouses by Act of Parliament. Initially they were required to build four lights, but many more followed; their first, at Kinnaird Head on the north-east coast, was lit in 1787. The powers of the Commissioners, who form the Northern Lighthouse Board, were extended to the Isle of Man in 1854, although they had already been granted permission to build two lights there in 1815. The Stevenson family provided a succession of Engineers to the Board, beginning with Robert Stevenson in 1799, and continuing with his sons Alan, David and Thomas and his grandson David Alan Stevenson, appointed in 1885; between them, they worked on over eighty lighthouses, including such well-known sites as Bell Rock, Muckle Flugga and Dubh Artach.

The lights of Ireland (Northern Ireland and the Republic) were the responsibility of a series of bodies, beginning with the Commissioners for Barracks in 1767. The Custom Board took over in 1796 and was followed by the Port of Dublin Authority, commonly known as the Ballast Board, in 1810. Finally, in 1867 the Commissioners of Irish Lights were created. George Halpin, Engineer to the Ballast Board during 1810–54, and his son George Halpin junior, who succeeded him, built over fifty lighthouses; many mid-nineteenth-century Irish lighthouses were their joint responsibility, as Halpin junior was assistant to his father from 1830.

A lighthouse was built on Longstone Rock, in the Farne Islands off Bamburgh, Northumberland, in 1810–11 to the design of Daniel Asher Alexander for Trinity House. The present Longstone lighthouse, a red and white banded circular stone tower 85 feet (26 metres) in height, was built by Joseph Nelson in 1827. The lighthouse was the home of Grace Darling in 1838, when she and her father, the lightkeeper, rescued nine survivors from the stricken 'Forfarshire'.

The first rock lighthouses

By the late seventeenth century the number of lighthouses around the coast of the British Isles had hardly increased from medieval times, although the emphasis in their location had moved from the south to the east coast of England, as trade across the North Sea and along its coasts became more important. Lighthouse design and construction were still relatively simple. Local materials were used where possible, to keep costs down, and the typical sixteenth- or seventeenth-century lighthouse was either a stone tower, often polygonal in cross-section, or a timber shelter on wooden columns.

The greatest steps in the evolution of lighthouse design and construction occurred between the end of the seventeenth century and the mid eighteenth century, when it became necessary to tackle the problem of building rock lights, those standing on small, wave-washed islets, often far from the coast. Overcoming the difficulties inherent in the construction of rock lights was one of the high points in the history of British civil engineering.

Conducting such a complex building operation on a tiny remote crag surrounded by the sea involved negotiating a sequence of hazards: reaching and landing on the rock, living on the rock during the short building season, ferrying materials to the site, and creating a structure strong enough to withstand the forces of wind and waves. These forces were much fiercer than

Pladda lighthouse stands on the island of Pladda, off the southern tip of Arran. It was built by Thomas Smith in 1790; the initial light was soon supplemented by a second light, displayed in a separate lantern 20 feet (6 metres) below the original lantern. This was to distinguish Pladda from three nearby lights. This system continued until 1901, when a flashing light was installed.

anything experienced in land-based construction and called for firm foundations and a massive weather-proof structure. Constant pounding by winter storms meant that joints between stones had to be impervious to driving water, while the lantern had to be placed well above the height reached by waves.

The earliest British rock light was built on Eddystone, three jagged ridges of rock in the English Channel, 13 miles (21 km) south-south-west of Plymouth. Huge seas break over the rocks, with the waves reaching nearly 100 feet (30 metres) in height. The need for the light became clear as the Atlantic shipping trade grew in importance, and in 1694 Trinity House began to search for a suitable builder. In effect, there was no precedent for the task of constructing a rock light. The only previous model, built on the shoal of Meloria, off Livorno on the north-west coast of Italy in 1157, was later destroyed and nothing is known of its design.

Godrevy lighthouse stands on Godrevy Island at the northern end of St Ives Bay, Cornwall. The octagonal white rubble-stone tower, 85 feet (26 metres) in height, was built by James Walker in 1859; it showed a white flashing light and a fixed red light that marked the Stones, a dangerous reef. Godrevy featured in Virginia Woolf's novel 'To the Lighthouse'.

Bardsey lighthouse stands on Bardsey Island, two miles across the rough waters of Bardsey Sound from the south-west tip of the Lleyn Peninsula. The lighthouse was built by Joseph Nelson in 1821 and has an unusual square cross-section; the red and white banded tower stands 99 feet (30 metres) high.

The challenge of building on Eddystone was eventually taken up by Henry Winstanley, an eccentric showman and businessman who had lost a ship on Eddystone. He began work in 1696, making twelve holes in the rock, into which iron stanchions would be fixed; this took an entire summer. During the following summer season the iron bars were put in place; these gave stability to the base of the tower, a solid stone drum measuring 16 feet (4.86 metres) in diameter. Above this, Winstanley erected a polygonal tower that contained the living quarters; the light was displayed from a lantern held by a dome at the top of the tower. It was first lit on 14th November 1698. During the following summer Winstanley strengthened the tower, widening the base and raising its height to 60 feet (18.3 metres), but on 26th November 1703 a storm swept the whole structure away, taking Winstanley with it.

The first Eddystone lighthouse was replaced in 1706–9 by a stone and timber tower designed by John Rudyerd, a silk merchant turned engineer. His tower was attached to the reef by means of thirty-six short wrought-iron stanchions, rammed into holes in the rock and secured with molten pewter, which cooled and hardened into a firm fitting. Holes in the iron bars enabled horizontal oak beams to be bolted on to the iron frame, forming a timber platform above which the 69 feet (21 metres) high tower was constructed. It stood until 2nd December 1755, when a fire, which began in the wooden lantern, burned it down. During the

The white tower of Davaar lighthouse stands on the north side of Davaar Island, at the entrance to Campbeltown Loch; a sandspit known as The Doirlinn separates the island from the mainland. The circular stone tower was built in 1854 by David and Thomas Stevenson.

47-year life of the second Eddystone lighthouse, a further three island lighthouses were built: Skerries, off Anglesey (1714–17), Casquets, off Alderney in the Channel Islands (1723–4), and Flatholm, in the Bristol Channel (1737). All were circular stone towers (there were three towers at Casquets, to distinguish it from other lighthouses), and all were lower in height than the Eddystone lights and stood in less challenging locations.

The construction of the third Eddystone lighthouse in 1756–9 was carried out by one of Britain's greatest lighthouse engineers, John Smeaton. He devised a system of interlocking masonry, whereby individual stone blocks at the base of the

Trwyn Du, off the eastern tip of the Isle of Anglesey, was the first wave-washed tower to be designed by James Walker. The circular stone 95 feet (29 metres) high tower was built in 1837–8 and has a stepped base, vertical walls and a battlemented parapet. The light, which works on solar power, gives a white flash every five seconds, and the fog signal is a bell.

Lismore lighthouse marks the eastern end of the Sound of Mull and can easily be seen from the Oban to Mull ferry. It stands on the little island of Eilean Musdile, which is attached to the much larger Lismore island by a single-arched bridge. The lighthouse was designed by Robert Stevenson and built in 1833; the keepers' accommodation is arranged symmetrically either side of the white, circular 102 feet (31 metres) high tower.

The upper part of Smeaton's Eddystone lighthouse, completed in 1759, now stands on Plymouth Hoe, Devon. John Smeaton (1724–92), a distinguished civil engineer, made the third attempt to erect a lighthouse on the dangerous Eddystone rocks, and his construction lasted until 1882, when it was replaced by a tower built by James Douglass. Smeaton used interlocking masonry in the construction of his tower, an innovative solution that was the model for many other lights.

tower could not be removed other than in the reverse order to their setting. The blocks, hewn into long zigzag shapes on their lateral edges, fitted closely together and at the centre of the tower interlocked with the rock itself, which had previously been prepared with dovetails. Horizontal shearing was avoided by the use of marble dowels, which slotted into holes made in adjoining stones, and long metal pins, which held the courses together. Smeaton also experimented with hydraulic mortar, which set under water.

Work on the rock began in August 1756 and the first stone, weighing 2.25 tons, was laid on 12th June 1757. During the first building season, nine courses of stone were laid; in the three years between the start of preparatory work and the first showing of the light on 16th October 1759 a total of only sixteen weeks of building work was possible.

Smeaton's lighthouse continued in use for 123 years; his use of dovetailing and interlocking masonry was a crucial stage in the development of lighthouse engineering. The circular cross-section of the tower lessened wind and wave resistance, while its elegantly tapered form resulted in a lower centre of gravity and greater stability. It also led the way in lighthouse architecture, as the designers of many land-based lights adopted

The interlocking construction method used by John Smeaton in the building of the third Eddystone lighthouse may be seen in a pavement display at the junction of Millbay Road and West Hoe Road in the Millbay Docklands area of western Plymouth. The cross-section also contains a lead nugget, a reminder of the fiery fate of John Rudyerd's second Eddystone. The pavement installation is part of the Waterfront Walkway, which follows the South West Coast Path through Plymouth.

The pair of lights at Mockbeggar (Leasowe) on the Wirral were built in 1763 by the Docks Committee of Liverpool Corporation and known as the Sea Lights. The outer light disappeared soon after it was erected, but the inner light remains; it was last lit in 1908. The lighthouse was bought by Wallasey Corporation for £900 in 1930 and restored at a cost of £30,000 during 1988–9; 132 new cast-iron steps (made to the original 1824 design) were installed in 1990. Leasowe lighthouse, a Grade II listed building, is Britain's oldest brick-built lighthouse.

the round tower format. Smeaton's innovations remained the basis of lighthouse construction throughout the nineteenth century.

Only four more rock lights were constructed in Britain before the end of the eighteenth century. Three were stone-built, but at the Smalls, off St Ann's Head in Pembrokeshire, Henry Whiteside (previously a musical-instrument maker) experimented with a small wooden tower fixed above wooden piles. The piles – vertical and near-vertical wooden stakes – formed an open structure, which presented less resistance to waves than solid masonry. The tower was built in 1776 and stood for eighty-five years, but required constant maintenance. By 1800, the coast of England was the best lit in Europe, although France was not far behind, with twenty lighthouses.

Lighthouse construction in the nineteenth century

The world's second great rock light, after Smeaton's Eddystone of 1756–9, was the stone tower erected in 1807–10 on Bell Rock, a sandstone plateau barely uncovered at low tide, sited 11 miles (18 km) off Arbroath on the east coast of Scotland. Bell Rock and the nearby rocky shore had always been a danger to ships trading in the Firths of Forth and Tay, and the loss of around seventy vessels in a series of violent storms in the area during 1799 forced the Northern Lighthouse Commissioners to tackle this most difficult construction problem.

Robert Stevenson, Engineer to the Northern Lighthouse Board during 1799–1842, began work on the foundations of Bell Rock in July 1807. He used a converted fishing boat named the *Pharos*, which was moored around 2 miles (3 km) off the rock, to house his workmen. This was replaced in 1808 by a barrack, which took a year to build; it was a 50 feet (15 metres) high beacon-shaped

The Signal Tower (1813), Arbroath, was the shore station for Bell Rock lighthouse, which stands 11 miles (18 km) off Arbroath and was first lit in 1811. The copper ball on top of the tower was used as a signal. Every morning the keeper at Signal Tower would look at the lighthouse through a telescope; if a similar ball there was raised, he would return the signal by raising the ball at the tower, but if the ball was not raised, he would have to go to the lighthouse. The four keepers worked a rota of six weeks on Bell Rock and two weeks ashore, with one changing over every fortnight. The Signal Tower was home to the lightkeepers and their families until 1955 and is now a museum.

The original coal-fired leading lights at Harwich, Essex, were erected in 1665; the low light was a wooden tower on the beach, while the high light was a lantern on top of the town gate. Both were rebuilt in 1817–18, and the High Lighthouse now stands on West Street. It is a nine-sided 90 feet (27 metres) high yellow-brick tower designed by Daniel Asher Alexander, Surveyor to Trinity House. After being made redundant in 1863, the lighthouse was sold to the local council in 1909, eventually becoming a private home.

structure supported by iron piles driven into the rock and was connected to the growing lighthouse tower by a bridge. The workmen stayed in the barrack during high-tide periods when work was impossible, thus maximising the available building time. Stevenson also laid an iron railway track from the highest landing point of the rock to the tower, to transport the huge pre-cut granite blocks shipped out from Arbroath.

At Bell Rock Stevenson improved on Smeaton's system of horizontally interlocking masonry blocks and central dovetailing by extending the dovetailing throughout each horizontal course, making the tower even more resistant to shearing forces. After four seasons of work, one lasting only twenty-two working days, the 100 feet (30.5 metres) high lighthouse tower was completed in August 1810 and came into service on 1st February 1811. The light, an oil lamp, could be seen from 25 miles (40 km) away in good visibility, and two large bells, powered by the same machinery that turned the light, gave a fog signal.

Encouraged by the success of Bell Rock (although the cost turned out to be 50 per cent more than the original estimate of £42,000), the Northern Lighthouse Board pushed ahead with a building programme that took in twelve Scottish sites and two on the Isle of Man, meeting few problems until the construction of Skerryvore, on jagged rocks 12 miles (19 km) west of Tiree,

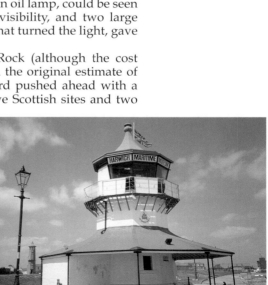

The Low Lighthouse, which stands on the Esplanade at Harwich, was built under the supervision of John Rennie senior in 1817–18; it is a ten-sided 45 feet (14 metres) high brick tower with a canopy around its base. Harwich High and Low lighthouses became redundant in 1863, because of the changing course of the channel, and were replaced by the Dovercourt lighthouses. Harwich Low Lighthouse, which is 450 feet (137 metres) from the High Lighthouse, became the Maritime Museum in 1980.

The cast-iron leading lights on (and just offshore from) Dovercourt's Central Promenade in Essex were built in 1863 to replace an earlier pair of lighthouses at nearby Harwich. The pair of Dovercourt lights were in turn made redundant when the channels shifted again in 1917. The iron-piled lights were restored in 1983–8.

between Ireland and the Hebrides.

Robert Stevenson's son Alan, Engineer to the Northern Lighthouse Board during 1843–53, was given the task of building Skerryvore. Work began in June 1838, but the whole summer's effort was lost in a winter storm; in the following year, gunpowder was used to blast foundations in the uneven surface. Alan Stevenson followed his father's building system only in the erection of a barrack; for the 158 feet (48 metres) high stone tower he dispensed with costly and time-consuming dovetailing and relied on dowelling in the outer courses of masonry to provide sufficient resistance to the waves. The surface of the reef stood above high water, in contrast to the wave-swept Bell Rock, and Stevenson calculated that the great weight of the tower would prevent stones being dislodged. The ten-storey lighthouse was ready for testing in September 1843 and came into service on 1st February 1844.

Alexander Gordon of London, a builder specialising in cast-iron structures, claimed that he could have designed an iron tower for Skerryvore at one-tenth the cost of the stone structure. The claim was refuted by Stevenson, who pointed to the fate of two nearby iron beacons that had been destroyed in storms, but mid-nineteenth-century enthusiasm for iron construction led to several iron lighthouses being built in less exposed situations.

A cast-iron harbour lighthouse was erected at Swansea as early as 1803, but the first iron lighthouse on an offshore site was built at Maplin Sands, off Foulness on the Essex coast, in 1838–41. The screwpile system patented by Alexander Mitchell in 1832, whereby iron castings fitted with screw blades were screwed into

Below: *The lighthouse at Coquet Island, off Amble, Northumberland, was built to the design of James Walker in 1839–41 on the remains of a fourteenth- or fifteenth-century tower house, once home to a cell of Benedictine monks. The lightkeeper's cottage stands on the site of their chapel.*

The tiny brass hand grasping a handle is typical Trinity House detailing; in this case the half-height door opens on to the lantern balcony at Souter lighthouse, County Durham. Keepers needed access to the outside of the lantern in order to clean the glass. The Souter staff comprised one engineer and four assistant lightkeepers, one of whom had to be in the lantern between sunset and sunrise.

the ground, was used at Maplin. Mitchell himself supervised the construction of the foundations, which consisted of nine wrought-iron legs driven into the sands by cast-iron screws. The superstructure, designed by James Walker, later a consultant engineer to Trinity House, consisted of a small platform and lantern. Mitchell was involved in the building of four other iron lighthouses during 1840–53.

The fate of the Fastnet lighthouse, a cast-iron tower erected on Fastnet Rock, off the south-west coast of Cork, by George Halpin junior in 1854, simply confirmed prevailing opinion among engineers that iron structures were cheaper than masonry towers but were useful only in less-exposed situations. The 92 feet (28 metres) high Fastnet tower was built up from flanged plate; the structure was found to tremble right from the start and, after attempts to strengthen it with concrete and masonry, it was eventually replaced in 1904.

During the late nineteenth century further advances were made in the construction of stone-built rock lights. The problem of water surging up the tower, as heavy seas broke over its base, was tackled by James Walker in the replacement of the wooden Smalls lighthouse, off the Pembrokeshire coast, which dated from 1776. Walker's design, produced in 1856, featured a stepped base to break up the force of the waves; the granite tower was built in 1858–61 by Nicholas and James Douglass.

Walker used the same idea at Wolf Rock, 8 miles (13 km) south-west of Land's End, erected in 1861–9 by Nicholas, James and William Douglass. Lights in Cornish waters posed even more intractable problems than those of Scotland, as the full force of the Atlantic swept across the sites, which were only small pinnacles of rock. There was no room for a

Below: *Wolf Rock lighthouse stands 8 miles (13 km) south-west of Land's End. The 135 feet (41 metres) high granite tower was erected in 1861–9 to the design of James Walker, and first lit in 1870. It was the first lighthouse to have a helideck constructed, in 1973, and was automated in 1988.*

Bidston lighthouse, about two miles from Liverpool Bay on Bidston Hill near Birkenhead, Wirral, was last lit regularly in 1913. The first lighthouse on the site, a 55 feet (17 metres) high octagonal tower, was built in 1771. This was replaced in 1872 by the surviving round stone tower, which stands slightly to the north of the original light. The lighthouse was briefly re-lit in October 2000 to mark the end of British Summer Time.

Pendeen lighthouse, on the Cornish coast 6 miles (10 km) north of Land's End, was built in 1900 and designed by Thomas Matthews, Trinity House Engineer. Within the white tower are two rooms topped by the lantern, which was originally lit by an Argand oil lamp; the lighthouse was converted to electricity in 1926. Pendeen was automated in 1995 and the three single-storey keepers' cottages are used as holiday accommodation.

St Mary's lighthouse, Whitley Bay, Northumberland, under construction in 1897–8, with scaffolding reaching to just below the level of the lantern. The main building materials were 645 blocks of local Heworth sandstone and 750,000 bricks. Construction was a simpler operation than at most rock lights, as materials could be brought in across the rocks at low tide, rather than having to be shipped to the site. The lighthouse was built by the firm of John Livingstone Miller of Tynemouth and cost £8000.

barrack, and building seasons were severely truncated.

James Douglass improved on Walker's stepped-base design during the rebuilding of Bishop Rock, west of the Isles of Scilly, in 1883–7. He produced a massive masonry drum, 41 feet (12.5 metres) across and 38 feet (11.6 metres) high, to encase the base of the old tower. It was effective in breaking up the seas, and the drum base soon became a normal part of lighthouse design.

The ultimate refinement of Smeaton's original central dovetailing, and the horizontal dovetailing introduced by Robert Stevenson at Bell Rock, came in 1861–2 at Les Hanois, a reef south-west of Guernsey. Here Nicholas Douglass used a combination of vertical and horizontal dovetailing in a tower of circular cross-section, giving a structure of stone blocks which

Above: *The 126 feet (38 metres) high white-painted circular brick tower of St Mary's lighthouse on St Mary's Island, Whitley Bay; its lantern was designed by Thomas Matthews, engineer-in-chief to Trinity House. The initial light source was paraffin, but the light was converted to electricity in 1977–8 and automated in 1979. The light was discontinued in 1984 and the fittings removed; the optic now at St Mary's was originally at Withernsea lighthouse. St Mary's lighthouse is owned by North Tyneside Council and is open to the public.*

Right: *The 137-step spiral stair of St Mary's lighthouse, Whitley Bay, leads up to the single internal floor beneath the lantern. The lighthouse marked the northern approach to the river Tyne and was first lit on 31st August 1898, when it was ceremonially opened by the Misses Miller and Wilson, the daughter and niece respectively of its builder, J. L. Miller. In the foreground is the light apparatus originally used at the 'East Goodwin' lightship, and now on display at St Mary's.*

interlocked with each other upwards, downwards and to both sides, a three-dimensional jigsaw of masonry. This technique, although costly and requiring great skill on the part of the masons, became the accepted technique for lighthouse construction.

By the late 1870s it had become apparent that masonry in the first rock light, Smeaton's Eddystone, was suffering from its constant pounding by wind and waves, and the decision was taken to commission a replacement. This lighthouse, the fourth Eddystone, was the greatest work of James Douglass, then Engineer-in-Chief to Trinity House. He used a specially built steamship to ferry out the cut granite blocks, each of which was

Early days in the construction of the fourth Eddystone lighthouse, in the English Channel 13 miles (21 km) south-west of Plymouth, Devon. The photograph was probably taken in 1879, as the tower, designed by James Douglass, was beginning to rise above its foundations. A massive granite block is being lifted into position on the right of the tower. To the left is Smeaton's tower, the third lighthouse on the site, built in 1756–9, the top of which now stands on Plymouth Hoe.

carried in the ship's hold on a wheeled bogie, ready to be lifted, run aft and hauled to the rock. The 168 feet (51 metres) high tower, comprising 2171 blocks, took only three and a half years to build, came in well under its original estimate and was lit on 18th May 1882. Douglass was knighted shortly afterwards.

Victorian lighthouse engineers produced innovative methods of construction and transport, and proved able to motivate their workers even during the worst weather conditions. Victorian lighthouse building reached such a peak of efficiency that few new developments took place in the early twentieth century, although concrete was gradually introduced after its first use at La Corbière, Jersey, in 1873–4, where it formed the core of a granite-faced tower.

La Corbière stands on a reef connected to the south-west coast of Jersey by a causeway that is impassable at high tide. It was built in 1873–4 and was Britain's first concrete lighthouse; although the core of the 62 feet (19 metres) high tower is concrete, the facing material is granite.

Showing the light

The basic source of light in the medieval lighthouse was a fire, burning wood, peat, reed bundles or possibly coal, which was held by an iron brazier. The fire was normally completely open to the elements, except where light was not required over a substantial sector of land, when a rear wall and roof might be provided. The dangers of fire spreading, combined with the difficulty of maintaining the fire in adverse weather conditions, led to experimentation with alternative light sources, candles and oil lamps, and the introduction of closed lanterns after glass became available in the thirteenth century.

However, the well-tended open fire, burning high-quality coal from the north of England, remained the most efficient light source until well into the eighteenth century. Such a light could be seen from a distance of around 7 miles (11.3 km), especially if the light was reflected by low cloud. The last open coal fire to be in use as a

This minor light, more lantern than lighthouse, stands on the cliffs near St Catherine's Point, overlooking the entrance to Fowey harbour in Cornwall. It may be seen from the coast path running westward between Fowey and the red and white striped Gribbin daymark on Gribbin Head.

Rinrawros Point or Aranmore lighthouse looks out over the Atlantic Ocean from Aran Island, off the north-west coast of Ireland. It is one of eighty major lighthouses maintained by the Commissioners for Irish Lights.

The lantern of Bardsey lighthouse, at the southern tip of Bardsey Island, off the north Wales coast; the lantern alone cost almost £3000 when the lighthouse was built by Trinity House in 1821. Its optic provides a white flash of light five times every 15 seconds, and the beam can be seen at a range of 26 sea miles. The lighthouse was automated in 1987.

light source at a British lighthouse was at St Bees, on the Cumbrian coast, in 1822.

Candles undoubtedly functioned as light sources in medieval lighthouses, but no details have survived. By the sixteenth century candles were being used to provide leading lights, which shone only in a narrow sector and guided mariners along a safe route, often into harbour. Leading lights were often built in pairs, as high and low lights, so that the towers could act as daymarks; mariners knew they were following the correct course if the towers were aligned vertically above one another. A single tallow candle was the source in a leading light built at North Shields, Northumberland, in 1539.

The candle was a surprisingly effective light source, particularly when used with a reflector; basic metal reflectors were introduced in other countries from the mid sixteenth century, but not until the eighteenth century in Britain. A candle provided the harbour light at Bridport, Dorset, as late as 1861. Candelabra were used where a stronger source was required; the light at the first Eddystone, Winstanley's tower of 1698, was a candelabrum of at least twenty-six candles.

Primitive oil lamps were also used as light sources in the medieval period; most common was the cresset, a hollowed-out stone filled with oil or fat and equipped with a simple wick. The oil was usually derived from vegetables or fish. Oil lamps were inefficient light sources until the introduction of the Argand lamp in 1784. The Swiss inventor Ami Argand designed a lamp with a hollow circular wick and a glass chimney, which controlled oil consumption and provided a good draught, thus creating a much brighter light. The Argand lamp became the standard light source by 1800. The fuel varied: sperm-whale oil was popular but herring oil, rape-seed oil and seal oil were also used, the choice often depending on price. Most of these oils were thick and flowed poorly, so when the cheap and volatile paraffin became available

An array of reflectors in the diminutive harbour lighthouse on the north bank of Mount Batten Point, Plymouth. The little peninsula, which divides the Cattewater (the mouth of the River Plym) from Plymouth Sound, was a sea-plane base during the First World War. The sheltered waters of the Sound were especially suitable for flying boats, the last of which took off from the Sound in 1952.

after about 1860 it was an immediate success and was the normal light source until the Second World War.

Lanterns evolved to protect the light source and lightkeepers from the elements but were inefficient until the eighteenth century because of the poor quality of the glass and light sources and the impossibility of keeping the glass clean in a smoky atmosphere. An early example was the pentagonal stone lantern, with three glazed windows, which existed on top of the church tower at St Michael's Mount in Cornwall in 1433. Here the light source was a cresset. During the seventeenth and eighteenth centuries attempts were made to enclose coal fires; a totally enclosed lantern, with glazing bars of lead-covered wood, was designed for the coal-burning lighthouse at St Agnes, Isles of Scilly, in 1680.

Parabolic reflectors were introduced towards the end of the eighteenth century. They overcame the problem of light rays inefficiently radiating upwards, downwards and landward from the source, rather than in the specific direction useful to mariners. Curved metal

In parabolic reflection, all light rays emanating from a light source placed at the focal point of the reflector and falling on its surface will be deflected into a single beam. The first efficient parabolic reflector was introduced by William Hutchinson, Dock Master of Liverpool, in 1763.

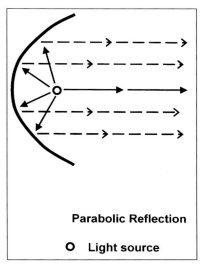

Parabolic Reflection

O Light source

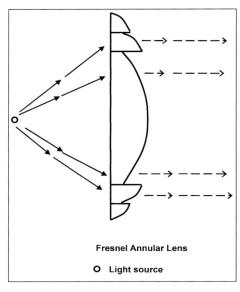

Fresnel Annular Lens

O **Light source**

The Fresnel annular lens, introduced in 1822, consisted of a central lens surrounded by ring lenses of differing curvature. The exact shape of the optic depended on the type of glass used and the nature of the expected light beam.

reflectors, normally 1 to 3 feet (0.5 to 1 metre) wide with parabolic cross-section, were placed behind the lamp, causing the rays of light to be reflected forwards in a single beam. Catoptric or reflecting systems could be complex, with a series of reflectors mounted side by side behind the light.

Refracting or dioptric systems involved the use of prisms and lenses. The prism is a glass of triangular cross-section that reflects or refracts light, depending on the direction of the incoming rays of light, while a lens concentrates light rays by refraction. In 1822 the Frenchman Augustin Fresnel invented the annular lens, a highly efficient optic in which a single lens was split into a central lens surrounded by concentric rings. As the edges of a lens were most ineffective in terms of distortion, this system avoided light wastage and concentrated the beam. One-third more light was found to be transmitted by dioptric than catoptric systems.

Lenses had been used, rather unsuccessfully, in lighthouse lanterns during the eighteenth century, as at South Foreland, Kent, in 1752, but Fresnel's system, introduced in 1823 to the lighthouse at Cordouan, an island off the Atlantic coast of France, near Bordeaux, was significantly more efficient. The next step was the combination of reflection and refraction in the catadioptric system, which used the reflective properties of the prism to produce the strength of beam necessary

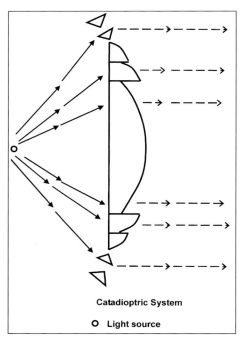

Catadioptric System

O **Light source**

The catadioptric system uses a Fresnel lens (centre) to refract light, in combination with rings of reflecting prisms (top and bottom). The rotation of a complex optic, consisting of several catadioptric lenses, around a light source produces a series of beams, seen by the mariner as a flashing light.

The double-height optic at Souter lighthouse, South Shields, County Durham. The original optic, installed in 1871 when the lighthouse was first lit, was an octagonal drum with seven lenses arranged vertically on each side. It was replaced by the present optic (left) in 1914, giving the light a range of over 20 miles (32 km). The optic is mounted on a turntable (above), the whole structure weighing around 4 tons (4064 kg). It rests on a bath of mercury; thus it can easily be turned, even by hand. The turntable was originally rotated by a weight-driven clockwork motor; a tube extending down the length of the tower held the weights, which had to be wound up by the lightkeeper every hour and a quarter. The view below, taken inside the double-height lenses at Souter, shows the ladder (beside the red lamp cover on the right) that provided access for the lightkeepers, who were able to work inside the apparatus even while it was rotating. The shoreward light was reflected downward through prisms and used in a secondary light, which appeared through a window in the tower.

for the new rock lights. In this apparatus, which became available after 1850, a Fresnel lens was surrounded by rings of prisms.

Differentiating lighthouses from one another had always been a problem. Different numbers of lights could be displayed at adjacent sites, although this was expensive and sometimes impractical, but the introduction of the complex optical apparatus provided a better solution. The optic could be rotated around the light source, each section of lenses producing a single beam. The mariner saw a pattern of light flashes, which could be varied by altering the number of lenses in the system and the speed of rotation. These optics could weigh around 3 tons, but towards the end of the nineteenth century it was realised that it was possible to float the optic on a bath of mercury, enabling the assembly to be turned with little effort.

Electricity was used as a light source from the second half of the nineteenth century. Trinity House first experimented with electricity at

The catadioptric apparatus (left) at St Mary's lighthouse, Whitley Bay, Northumberland. The central lens refracts light from the source, while the partial rings of prisms above and below it reflect light, producing a concentrated beam. The whole apparatus comprises eight lens assemblies mounted on an octagonal base; it would normally have been floated on a bath of mercury. When the apparatus is rotated, a separate beam is given out by each of the eight sections. This apparatus, which weighs 2.5 tons (2540 kg), was moved to St Mary's in 1988; its original home was Withernsea lighthouse, which was discontinued in 1976. The interior of the present optic at St Mary's lighthouse is shown below left. The original optic was a catadioptric apparatus, which gave out a beam visible 17 miles (27 km) out to sea and which flashed twice every 20 seconds. Its light complemented that of Souter lighthouse, to the south of the Tyne, and took the place of an old lighthouse at the mouth of the Tyne. The turning mechanism in the lighthouse (below right) is just below the optic and light source. In order that mariners could distinguish one lighthouse from another, their lights needed to show characteristic colours or intervals between flashes. To produce a flashing beam, the optic was rotated continuously by the turning gear, causing the light beams to move constantly round; to a mariner at sea, this gave the impression of a flashing light.

Dungeness lighthouse (1961) was the first to use the xenon electric arc lamp as its light source. There are four banks of four sealed beam units that give off a single white flash every 10 seconds; the range of the light is 27 miles (43 km). The panel of sixteen lamps revolves on a turntable. No lens is required, and the assembly is around a tenth of the weight of a traditional optic.

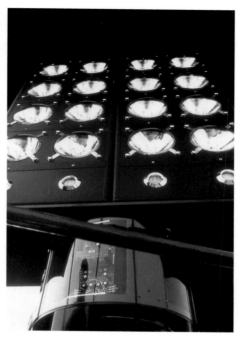

Dungeness in 1862, but the steam engines that powered the generators required constant stoking and the equipment was replaced in 1875. South Foreland, Kent, was the first lighthouse to use mains power and in 1922 became the first to be lit by a filament lamp.

The xenon discharge lamp, introduced in 1947, gave a light over forty times stronger than a filament lamp, but the most popular light source for modern lighthouses is the sealed beam unit, similar to those used in car headlights. An assembly of these units is relatively cheap, lightweight and needs no lens assembly. Looking to the future, Trinity House continues to evaluate alternative light sources including lasers.

The lightkeeper and the modern lighthouse

During the mid twentieth century advances in concrete technology allowed alterations to the traditional form of the lighthouse. The lighthouse built at Dungeness, Kent, in 1904 was replaced in 1961 by a slender reinforced concrete tower measuring only 12 feet (3.6 metres) across. Concrete caissons (hollow waterproof structures) were also found useful in the replacement of lightships by towers.

The world's earliest lightship, a small sailing ship, was stationed at Nore Bank, off Sheerness, Kent, in 1732. Purpose-built light-vessels were constructed after the 1820s, with the light normally shown from the mainmast; a central latticework tower, which carried the light, was introduced during the late nineteenth century. This arrangement allowed the optic to revolve around the light source, as in a fixed lighthouse. The modern light-vessel is steel-hulled, with the

The first lighthouse on the shingle flats at Dungeness was built in 1615; a second was erected in 1635, after the receding sea had left the old light too far from the water's edge. The same problem caused the construction of a third lighthouse, a 120 feet (37 metres) high tower, by Samuel Wyatt in 1792; the design was based on Smeaton's Eddystone. Later, lightkeepers' quarters were built to a drum-shaped plan around the base of Wyatt's tower. Although this lighthouse was taken down in 1904, when the fourth lighthouse was lit, the houses remained standing beside the new tower (above). The fourth lighthouse, a 135 feet (41 metres) high brick tower, was built during 1901–4; now all black, it was originally painted in black and white bands to act as a daymark. Obscured by the construction of a nuclear power station nearby, it was succeeded in 1961 by a slim concrete tower (right) 141 feet (43 metres) high, with integral black and white bands. The spiral ramp at its base is part of the structure of the tower and does not lead to its entrance. The honeycomb section near the top of the tower conceals fog-warning equipment. The lighthouse was automated in 1991.

The 'Spurn' lightship, now moored in Hull Marina and open to the public. A floating light was stationed at New Sand, off Spurn Head at the mouth of the Humber estuary, in 1820. It survived less than a year, and in 1832 a wooden light-vessel was moored at Bull Sand, further into the estuary; this was replaced by an iron-built ship in 1847, but it suffered from frequent collisions with boats. The Spurn lightship was built in 1927 and stationed at New Sand in the same year; it was moved to Bull Sand in 1959 and decommissioned in 1975. The lantern stands 35 feet (11 metres) above the waterline.

lantern supported by a hollow steel mast.

The *Kish Bank* light-vessel in Dublin Bay was replaced in 1965 by a concrete caisson-type tower, which was built in Dun Laoghaire harbour, towed off the coast and sunk on to the site. Sand was pumped in to fill the caisson, then the watertight inner tower was floated upwards and secured with concrete. Its final height was 110 feet (33.5 metres). In a similar operation the *Royal Sovereign* light-vessel, 8 miles (13 km) east of Beachy Head, East Sussex, was replaced by a tower in 1970–1.

The daily duties of the lightkeeper, whether ashore, at rock stations or aboard light-vessels, revolved around cleaning and maintaining the light and the fog signals. On rock stations the normal complement of crew was three, each man working an

A high stone wall helps to protect the keepers' accommodation at Souter lighthouse, County Durham, from the elements. The lighthouse, built in 1870–1, needed a good water supply for its boilers, but the site had neither streams nor springs, so huge rainwater tanks capable of holding 60,000 gallons (272,760 litres) were incorporated into the foundations of the inner courtyard and engine room.

The houses and offices at Souter lighthouse as seen from the lantern balcony. Six separate keepers' houses, each with its own walled front garden, the engine room and various storerooms were laid out around a courtyard with a covered inner corridor. Each house had a kitchen and parlour downstairs, and two bedrooms upstairs; adjacent houses had interconnecting doors, giving some flexibility in accommodation.

eight-hour shift once every twenty-four hours. Around the end of the eighteenth century at the Smalls lighthouse, off the Pembrokeshire coast, one of the two lightkeepers was accidentally killed during a storm. His fellow keeper preserved the body for over two weeks until the relief arrived, in case he should be suspected of murder. Thereafter a third keeper was added to the crew at rock stations.

Lightkeepers alternated four weeks ashore and four weeks at the light, with a total of six keepers allocated to each rock station to allow for periods of shore leave. At shore stations and the larger island stations the keepers and their families lived permanently at the lighthouse, usually in accommodation connected to or sited close by the light.

A typical day's work for the late-nineteenth- or twentieth-century lightkeeper involved cleaning the optic and the windows of the lantern, taking meteorological readings, keeping watch and tending the machinery used to turn the optic. This clockwork mechanism was normally driven by a weight falling slowly from the top to the bottom of the tower. The weight had to be wound up about every half-hour, an onerous task for the keeper on duty at night, whose main job was to ensure the light was operating correctly.

The lantern windows had to be kept clean in all weathers, including snowstorms, when snow

The original foghorn at Souter lighthouse, County Durham, was a single, white-painted horn facing straight out to sea. This was replaced first by a pair of horns, angled to project the sound up and down the coast, and then by a pair of larger, black horns, which gave a four-second blast every 45 seconds and were powered by compressed air generated in the engine room. The interior of the foghorn house had elaborate glazed tile decoration.

Outside the lantern at Souter lighthouse; the handles enabled the lightkeepers to hold on to the lantern while cleaning the glass panes. Ladders could be hung from the protruding spikes. The tower is painted white with a single red band, the lantern also being red, although the technical term for the colour of the 'red' paint is International Orange.

Right: The keepers' accommodation at Ardnamurchan lighthouse on the Point of Ardnamurchan in Scotland, the most westerly point of the British mainland. The 118 feet (36 metres) high grey Mull granite tower was built by Alan Stevenson in 1849.

sticking to the glass could obscure the light. Access to the outside of the lantern was usually through a hinged section of the glass. The keeper climbed a ladder attached to a ridge running around the top of the lantern in order to reach the uppermost sections of glass. In bad weather this was one of the keeper's most hazardous tasks. In the days of coal braziers the keepers continually had to haul coal up the winding stairs of the lighthouse to the lantern.

For rock and island stations communication with the shore was vital. Before the days of radio and telephone visual methods such as flags, or a varying number of discs displayed on poles, were the norm, although pigeon post was used at Ailsa Craig, an island station off the south-west coast of Scotland.

A decorative detail from the Northern Lighthouse Board's Port St Mary shore station for the Chicken Rock lighthouse off the south-west tip of the Isle of Man. The houses replaced the previous shore station, actually the old keepers' accommodation for the two lights on the Calf of Man island, abandoned when the Chicken Rock light was lit in 1875.

St Bees lighthouse stands on the sheer cliffs of St Bees Head, south of Whitehaven in Cumbria. The first lighthouse on the site, a coal-burning 30 feet (9 metres) high tower probably made from local sandstone, was built in 1718 but burned out in 1822. Its replacement, a 56 feet (17 metres) high white-painted stone tower, was built in the same year by Joseph Nelson. The new light was oil-burning; St Bees was the last coal-fired lighthouse in Britain. It was converted to automatic working in 1987 and the adjoining cottages sold by Trinity House in 1988.

Walney lighthouse overlooks Morecambe Bay from the southern tip of Walney Island, which is connected to mainland Cumbria by a bridge at Barrow-in-Furness. A light, supported by a wooden tower, was first shown on the site in 1790, but the structure was destroyed by fire in 1803. The present white-painted octagonal 70 feet (21 metres) high tower was built in 1804 using stone quarried at Overton, near Lancaster. The light was improved in 1820 when four silver-plated copper reflectors, designed by Robert Stevenson, were installed. The present reflectors, although not original, constitute one of the last catoptric or reflecting systems still in use. The lighthouse is owned and run by the Port of Lancaster Commissioners.

The present (fourth) Eddystone lighthouse, a 161 feet (49 metres) high tower built by James Douglass in 1878–82 off Plymouth, Devon. Nearby is the stump of Smeaton's tower, the third Eddystone lighthouse, built in 1756–9. The upper part of Smeaton's tower now stands on Plymouth Hoe. The light gives a white flash twice every 10 seconds. Its automation was completed on 18th May 1982, exactly 100 years after its opening; Eddystone was the first Trinity House rock lighthouse to be automated.

Keepers generally had seafaring or engineering backgrounds and normally served four or five years at a series of stations during a career in the service. Their employers encouraged the keepers to see themselves as public servants, with responsibility for the safety of ships and mariners. Falling asleep when on watch was the greatest offence a keeper could commit. On rock stations, apart from the peculiar demands of living in what a modern keeper has described as an upright tube, the weather has always made the job hazardous. A mountainous wave was probably responsible for the tragedy that occurred at the remote

The Groyne lighthouse on the South Groyne at the mouth of the Tyne in South Shields. The striking red octagonal lighthouse was built by the local Trinity House Board in 1882; the cast-iron superstructure is supported by iron pilings. The South Groyne is open to the public, although the lighthouse itself is not.

Flannan Islands lighthouse, 15 miles (24 km) west of the Outer Hebrides, on 15th December 1900. All three keepers disappeared, apparently swept away as they were working at the spot where relief boats landed.

With the advent of electricity and diesel generators from the 1920s and 1930s the duties of the lightkeeper eventually became less time-consuming. A foretaste of the most momentous change in the British lighthouse service came in 1922, when the first conversion of a Trinity House lighthouse to fully automatic working took place. The light concerned was Trwyn Du, on the north-east coast of Anglesey.

Lighthouse automation, with remote control of light and fog signal, gathered pace after the Second World War, and Trinity House ceased to recruit keepers in 1980. In 1982 Eddystone became the first of their rock stations to be converted to automatic working. By 1993 the Corporation controlled only thirty-two manned lights, and all their lighthouses were automated by the end of 1998.

The same process has taken place around the entire coastline of the British Isles. Regular visits from engineers are now carried out using helicopters, which drop down on to landing pads built above the lanterns. The lighthouses themselves, particularly those on more accessible sites, are also becoming redundant, as sophisticated electronic navigation aids – radar beacons (racons), radio beacons and satellite systems – take over from visual warnings. The lighthouse structures still remain, however, as a monument to the skill of their builders. Their survival depends on finding alternative uses; several have been turned into private homes or hotels, while others are in the care of preservation trusts.

A selective gazetteer of British and Irish lighthouses

Note: there are some lighthouses illustrated elsewhere in this book but not listed here; they can be found by referring to the index.

CHANNEL ISLANDS

Casquets, west of Alderney. Unique British lighthouse as it originally had three separate lights (St Peter, St Thomas and Dungeon, all lit 1724) on the same site to aid identification. Of the three towers, the most westerly, painted in red and white horizontal bands, now holds the light.

La Corbière, south-west tip of Jersey. Concrete tower built in 1873–4. (See page 24.)

Les Hanois, reef off south-west tip of Guernsey. Built of Cornish granite in 1861–2 by Nicholas Douglass, using an innovative combination of vertical and horizontal dovetailing.

Point Robert, east coast of Sark. The lighthouse (1912–13) is set into the cliffs; the short octagonal tower stands on top of the keeper's accommodation.

Quénard Point, north-east tip of Alderney. The white lighthouse, with a broad black band, was built in 1912; the tapered tower stands 105 feet (32 metres) high.

ENGLAND
CHESHIRE

Bidston Hill, Birkenhead, SJ 287899. Last lit 1913. (See page 22.)

Hoylake, Valentia Road, SJ 214891. Pair of lights, last lit 1886 (upper) and 1908 (lower).

Above: *The pair of lighthouses known as the Lake Light were erected at Hoylake in 1763; they marked the entrance t Hoyle Lake, which then separated Hoyle Sands from th mainland of what is now the Wirral. Both towers we. replaced in 1865. The lower light ceased to function in 190 and was mostly demolished, but the upper light, whic operated until 1886, still stands complete with its fir wrought-iron staircase. The lighthouse is now part of private home that includes the adjoining two keeper cottages.*

Left: *New Brighton (Perch Rock) lighthouse, just north Black Rock fort, was designed by John Foster, Liverpo Corporation Surveyor, and built in 1827–30. The 63 feet (1 metres) high tower is made from Anglesey granite and is sol for the first 36 feet (11 metres), with three floors of livir accommodation and the lamp room above. The light was ke by two keepers, alternately working three days on shore ar four in the lighthouse, until 1925, when it was automate New Brighton was last lit in 1963 and the tower becam privately owned in 1973.*

Near right: *Tater Du lighthouse stands on a small headland just west of Lamorna Cove, on the south coast of Cornwall. The 49 feet (15 metres) high tower was built by Trinity House in 1965, using white concrete blocks. It has always been an automatic station, with the main light showing three white flashes every 15 seconds, as well as a red sector light warning shipping of the Runnelstone Rocks.*

Above right: *The Barrow Monument, on the summit of Hoad Hill, which commands the town of Ulverston in Cumbria, was built in 1850 to commemorate the locally born geographer Sir John Barrow (1764–1848), Secretary of the Admiralty. The 100 feet (30 metres) tall limestone seamark, designed by the architect Andrew Trimen, resembles Smeaton's Eddystone lighthouse. The lantern's pilasters are engraved with the names of Arctic explorers. The monument was restored during 1990–2 and is occasionally open to the public.*

Leasowe, east of Hoylake, SJ 914253. Last lit 1908. (See page 17.)
New Brighton, on Perch Rock just north of the fort, SJ 309947. Built 1827–30.

CORNWALL
Bishop Rock, 4 miles (6 km) west of the Scilly Isles, SV 807065. James Walker built a wrought-iron screwpile lighthouse on Bishop Rock in 1847–9; never lit as washed away during 1850 storm. Walker then designed a granite tower for the rock, built 1851–8 by James Douglass. Reconstructed by James Douglass 1883–7 after damage to its base; round tower 167 feet (51 metres) high.
Godrevy, island in St Ives Bay, SW 577436. Built 1859. (See page 12.)
Lizard, Lizard Point, SW 705116. Originated with twin towers built 1752. (See page 8.)
Longships, 1 mile (2 km) west of Land's End, SW 320253. First lighthouse was a circular 79 feet (24 metres) high tower, built by Samuel Wyatt 1794–5, but waves washed over the lantern in storms and a new grey granite tower was built beside the old tower in 1873 by James Douglass.
Pendeen, north of St Just, SW 378359. Built 1900. (See page 22.)
Round Island, northern tip of Isles of Scilly, SV 902178. A low tower on a small islet, built in 1887 by William Douglass; shows a red light.
St Anthony's, eastern entrance to Falmouth harbour, SW 846312. White, octagonal 62 feet (19 metres) high tower built 1834–5 by Trinity House to a design by James Walker.
Tater Du, headland west of Lamorna Cove, SW 440231. Built 1965.
Trevose Head, west of Padstow, SW 851766. White 89 feet (27 metres) high round tower built 1845–7 by Jacob and Thomas Olver of Falmouth to a design by James Walker.
Wolf Rock, south-west of Land's End, SW 269120. Daymark built on this single granite pinnacle 1795, then beacon built by James Walker 1836–40. Present lighthouse designed by James Walker and built 1861–9, lit 1870; light gives white flash once every 15 seconds. (See page 21.)

CUMBRIA
St Bees, south of Whitehaven, NX 942144. First lit 1718. (See page 36.)
Walney, on Walney Island, south of Barrow-in-Furness, SD 230621. Built 1804. (See page 36.)

Lundy Old lighthouse is the highest lighthouse in Britain, standing on Chapel Hill, the highest point of Lundy Island, at 567 feet (173 metres) above sea level. The elegant 96 feet (29 metres) high tower was built from massive pale granite blocks, quarried locally. (Above) The view from the lantern. (Left) The stone spiral staircase inside the lighthouse, which is now a holiday home in the care of the Landmark Trust. The two-storey stone-built keepers' accommodation is still divided into the original upper and lower flats.

DEVON

Berry Head, east of Brixham, SX 946567. Lighthouse (1906) is white lantern on 200 feet (61 metres) high headland; highest (and possibly smallest) mainland lighthouse.

Bull Point, 4 miles (6 km) west of Ilfracombe, SS 462469. First lighthouse built 1879, damaged 1972 by cliff fall. Temporary tower (from Braunton Sands) used until permanent replacement lit 1974.

Eddystone, rock 13 miles (21 km) south-west of Plymouth, SX 383337. First lighthouse built 1696–8; demolished in storm 1703. Second lighthouse erected 1706–9; burned down 1755. John Smeaton's lighthouse of 1756–9 was in use for 123 years; upper section now stands on Plymouth Hoe. Present lighthouse built 1878–82 by James Douglass. (See pages 15, 16, 24, 36.)

Lundy North lighthouse, at the northern tip of Lundy Island, was one of two lighthouses built in 1897 to replace the old lighthouse; its white tower is 53 feet (16 metres) high. Lundy Island was taken on by the National Trust in 1969.

The white 56 feet (17 metres) high tower of Lundy South lighthouse (1897) is perched on the cliffs at the southern end of Lundy Island, overlooking the ferry landing stage; it was automated in 1994. The island has a permanent population of about eighteen.

Hartland Point, north of Bude, SS 230278. White 59 feet (18 metres) high tower built 1874 by James Douglass.

Lundy Island, Bristol Channel. First lighthouse, SS 133443, built 1819–20; Lundy North, SS 131482, and Lundy South, SS 144437, both built 1897.

Lynmouth Foreland, Foreland Point, east of Lynton, SS 754513. White 49 feet (15 metres) high tower built 1900, site cut into headland with 60 feet (18 metres) high retaining wall to rear.

Start Point, east of Salcombe, SX 829372. White 92 feet (28 metres) high tower built by James Walker 1836; battlemented balcony. Originally had two lights, one revolving and one fixed. Optic designed by Alan Stevenson. As with other Trinity House stations, keepers' accommodation in tower replaced by substantial house in walled enclosure 1871.

DORSET

Anvil Point, south of Swanage, SZ 029769. White-painted 39 feet (12 metres) high round tower built 1881 from local stone.

Portland Bill, southern tip of Isle of Portland, SY 677683. Two lighthouses lit 1716, one rebuilt 1789 by Trinity House and Argand lamps installed (the first at an English lighthouse). White-painted 23 feet (7 metres) high stone obelisk (seamark) built 1844, extant. New high and low lights built 1869 (extant), replaced 1906 with single 135 feet (41 metres) high white tower with broad red band. Shows white light with varying character, one to four flashes.

DURHAM

Heugh, Hartlepool, NZ 533339. First lighthouse built 1846, gas-lit; demolished 1915. Present lighthouse built 1926 using steel panelling.

Souter, Lizard Point, south of South Shields, NZ 408643. Built 1870–1. (See pages 29, 33, 34, 35.)

ESSEX

Dovercourt, TM 253308 and TM 254308. Pair of leading lights built 1863. (See page 20.)

Harwich, Low Lighthouse, TM 263324, and High Lighthouse, TM 262325. Built 1817–18. (See page 19.)

HAMPSHIRE

Hurst Point, on the Solent south of Lymington, SZ 318899. Low lights built 1866 and 1911, high light built 1867. (See page 42.)

The first lighthouse at Hurst Point, Hampshire, was built for Trinity House in 1785–6 and designed by Richard Jupp, surveyor to the East India Company. This low light stood south-west of Hurst Castle but was found to be obscured when viewed from particular angles, and a high light was added in 1812 by Daniel Alexander. Major additions were made to the castle during 1865–73, when both lights were re-sited, the low light as part of the fortification. A new low light, a squat circular granite tower (above left, in background), was built in 1866 and was itself replaced with the red-painted metal low lighthouse in 1911. The latter two lights still stand, although the low lighthouse was painted grey in 1997 (above left, foreground) in order to avoid it being mistaken for a daymark. The high lighthouse was replaced in 1867 with an 85 feet (26 metres) high white tower (above right). This was modernised in 1997, and, as well as showing the main light from its lantern, also projects green, red and white directional lights that can easily be realigned according to the movements of sandbanks in the Solent.

ISLE OF WIGHT

Needles, western end of Isle of Wight, SZ 289848. First light on nearby cliff-top built 1786 by Richard Jupp. Present lighthouse erected 1857–9 at end of Needles by James Walker; untapered 102 feet (31 metres) high granite tower, white with red band.

St Catherine's, southern tip of Isle of Wight, SZ 498755. First lighthouse on St Catherine's Hill (highest point of island) erected early fourteenth century, rebuilt *c.*1323; still stands (at SZ 494773), in care of English Heritage. Squat, stone tower partly built nearby as replacement in 1785, designed by Richard Jupp, but never completed. Present lighthouse at St Catherine's Point, a three-storey castellated octagonal tower of white-painted stone, built by James Walker 1838–40; lowered 1875 as lantern often obscured by mist. Fog signal added in attached tower (also battlemented) 1932, giving rise to the light's nickname, the Cow and Calf.

KENT

Dungeness, near Lydd, TR 094158. Present lighthouse built 1961. (See pages 31, 32.)

North Foreland, Broadstairs, TR 398696. Built 1691. (See page 6.)

South Foreland, north-east of Dover, TR 359434. Two wooden lighthouses erected 1636, replaced *c.*1719 by octagonal brick towers; both rebuilt 1793, but front tower abandoned *c.*1832. Rear (high) lighthouse is a white, castellated irregular octagonal tower, rebuilt 1843 and sold by Trinity House 1988; now in care of National Trust.

The lower lighthouse in Fleetwood, Lancashire, has a square base supporting a short square tower topped by an octagonal lantern. Both this lower light and the upper light or Pharos in Pharos Place, were probably designed by Decimus Burton (who planned Fleetwood); they were both lit in 1840. The upper light is a tall red sandstone column built in 1836–40, while the lower light, about a quarter of a mile (400 metres) away beside the beach, was built in 1836–41 on the Esplanade.

LANCASHIRE
Fleetwood, SD 339484. Upper and lower lights, lit 1840.

LINCOLNSHIRE
South Killingholme, TA 178183. Killingholme High light established 1831, rebuilt 1876–7, six-storey red 78 feet (24 metres) high tower. Killingholme South Low light, 45 feet (14 metres) high white tower, built 1836 for Trinity House by Francis Dales. These two lights lead shipping through the main Humber channel. Killingholme North Low light, white tower built 1851 by William Foale, signal station for Hull trawlers, redundant 1920, now a private home.

LONDON
Bow Creek, TQ 395807. The lighthouse at Trinity Buoy Wharf, near Orchard Place, Tower Hamlets, was built 1864–6 with the adjoining Chain and Buoy Store by James Douglass. It was one of a pair used by Trinity House in lighting trials; the other, on the west end of the Store, survived until the 1920s. The brick-built, 57 feet (17 metres) high tower stands on the west bank of Bow Creek where it enters the Thames. (See page 3.)

NORFOLK
Cromer, eastern edge of Cromer, TG 231416. Built 1833.

Sir John Clayton built a lighthouse at Foulness (now a shoal), off Cromer, Norfolk, in 1690, but it was never lit. An octagonal brick tower, lit by a coal fire, was built in Cromer in 1717, but constant erosion forced it to be abandoned in 1833, and the tower eventually disappeared in a cliff fall during 1866. This white-painted octagonal stone tower was erected in 1833, standing 58 feet (18 metres) high.

A wooden beacon, reputed to have been 100 feet (30 metres) in height, was built at Hunstanton, Norfolk, in 1550 to assist shipping entering the Wash. A pair of leading lights was erected in 1665, but only the high light functioned from 1750 onward, and this was burned out in 1777. The present lighthouse, designed by Ezekiel Walker, was built in 1778; it was rebuilt around 1830 but abandoned in 1921. Only one of the original pair of keepers' pitched-roofed cottages survives.

*High and low lights were built at Happisburgh, Norfolk, 1790–1 by William Wilkins the elder and Richard Norris; the lo_ light was demolished in 1883 but the high light, a red and whi_ banded 89 feet (27 metres) high tower with 112 steps, remained_ service until discontinued by Trinity House in 1987. T_ Happisburgh Lighthouse Trust then took over the running of t_ light; a special Act of Parliament, the Happisburgh Lighthou_ Act, was passed in 1990 to allow the light to be privately operate_*

Happisburgh, south of the village, TG 384307. Built 1790–1.

Hunstanton, northern edge of Hunstanton, TF 676420. Built 1778.

NORTHUMBERLAND

Coquet, on Coquet Island, off Amble, NU 293045. Built to the design of James Walker in 1839–41 on the remains of a fourteenth- or fifteenth-century tower house, itself constructed to defend a cell of Benedictine monks. Castellated sandstone 72 feet (22 metres) high tower is square and partly white-painted; light shows red to landward and white to seaward, flashing three times every 20 seconds. (See page 20.)

Farne, Inner Farne Island, NU 218358. First lighthouse on the island built 1673 by Sir John Clayton, although never lit. Private light erected 1778, then new lighthouse built for Trinity House by Joseph Nelson to

Bamburgh lighthouse, Northumberland, stands just north of Bamburgh village on low cliffs above Harkness Rocks. The white 30 feet (9 metres) high tower, which was built in 1910 using a cast-iron lattice construction system, is the most northerly land-based lighthouse in England.

Right: The old high lighthouse at Blyth, Northumberland, was built in 1788. The circular stone tower now stands among houses at some distance from the sea, as ballast-dumping has extended the shoreline eastward over the years. The lighthouse was the subject of a drawing by L. S. Lowry in 1970.

the design of Daniel Asher Alexander in 1810–11. The circular, white 43 feet (13 metres) high tower shows a white light to landward and a red light to seaward, flashing twice every 15 seconds.

Longstone, Farne Islands, NU 246390. Built 1827. (See page 11.)

St Mary's, St Mary's Island, Whitley Bay, NZ 353755. Built 1897–8. (See pages 22, 23, 30.)

SOMERSET

Burnham, north end of Burnham-on-Sea, ST 304506. A pair of leading lights was built privately at Burnham in 1801 to guide ships up the river Parrett to the port of Bridgwater. Trinity House took over the lease in 1829, and Joseph Nelson built new high and low lighthouses in 1832. The high light, a circular white-painted 99 feet (30 metres) high tower, is marooned amid houses, while the low light, a red and white wooden cabin supported by piles, stands on the beach.

The New High Light, Tyne Street, North Shields (right), was designed by the architect John Stokoe and built in 1808 for Trinity House of Newcastle upon Tyne, as was its companion the New Low Light, down below on Union Quay (below). The elegant stone tower of the New High Light has classical detailing and an iron balustrade around the lantern; the Old High Light (1727) is nearby. The New Low Light assisted mariners in finding safe passage into the river Tyne by correctly aligning it with the New High Light sited on the cliff above. The new lighthouses replaced an older pair of lights, rendered redundant when shifting sandbanks altered the position of the deepest channel. The first North Shields low light was erected in 1539, and the Old Low Light, built in 1727, still stands nearby. The new lighthouses were eventually replaced by pierhead lights in the late nineteenth century.

Southwold lighthouse, built in 1887–90, stands in the centre of the small Suffolk resort and guides shipping into the town's harbour. Its construction, under the supervision of James Nicholas Douglass, was a consequence of the loss of the low light at nearby Orfordness during a storm in 1887. The 102 feet (31 metres) high tower carries a main white light and two red sector lights.

SUFFOLK

Lowestoft, Yarmouth Road, TM 552944. Built 1874. (See page 7.)

Orfordness, on spit south of Aldeburgh, TM 449489. Two temporary lights (later replaced by wooden towers) were built by John Meldrum in 1635; two brick towers were erected in 1720. New high and low lights were built in 1792–3, the high light (the present lighthouse) being designed by William Wilkins the elder, a Norwich architect. The low light was lost after a storm in 1887. The circular 98 feet (30 metres) high tower is white with two red bands, the latter dating from 1867 alterations.

Southwold, TM 510763. Built 1887–90.

SUSSEX

Beachy Head, near Eastbourne, TV 582951. Replaced Belle Tout, built 1900–2.

Belle Tout, near Eastbourne, TV 564955. Built 1828.

Right: The first official lighthouse was built on Beachy Head, Sussex, at Belle Tout, about 2 miles (3 km) west of the highest point, in 1826–8, although beacons and small warning lights had been displayed on the headland from around 1670. The design, by James Walker for Trinity House, was finalised by the Sussex architect William Hallett. The squat, circular granite tower was decommissioned in 1902 because of fears of cliff erosion and difficulties with fog obscuring the light. To protect the building from cliff falls, Belle Tout lighthouse was moved 50 feet (15 metres) inland during 1999 in a complex engineering operation.

Left: The present Beachy Head lighthouse, at th foot of the cliffs just east of Belle Tout, was bui in 1900–2 by Sir Thomas Matthews. Th Cornish granite tower is sited about 541 fe (165 metres) seaward of the cliffs and stands 14 feet (43 metres) high. Electrification of the lig in 1974–5 involved carrying the mains supp via cables stretching from the cliff top to th tower; to discourage low-flying aircraft, th cables were marked by large red plastic balls intervals along their length. The light, whic shows two white flashes every 20 seconds, w automated in 1982.

Above and right: *The most recent lighthouse to be built on Spurn Head, East Yorkshire, is the 120 feet (37 metres) high brick tower put up by Sir Thomas Matthews for Trinity House in 1893–5. It was converted to automatic working in 1957 and decommissioned in 1985. Stone steps with iron railings lead up to the doorway, while the painted relief panel above bears the Trinity House arms, crest and motto 'Trinitas in Unitate'. The tower, painted in black and white bands, still functions as a daymark.*

YORKSHIRE, EAST

Flamborough, Flamborough Head, TA 254707. Old lighthouse built 1674, never lit; present lighthouse built 1806. (See pages 7, 8.)

Spurn Head, TA 403113. High light built 1893–5, decommissioned 1985; low light built 1771–6, rebuilt 1852, decommissioned 1895. (See page 9.)

Withernsea, TA 339280. Built 1892–3. (See page 1.)

YORKSHIRE, NORTH

South Gare, South Gare Breakwater, Redcar, NZ 558284. The small white lighthouse, which stands at the end of the breakwater, was lit in 1884. It was built of cast iron, copper and concrete by John Fowler, engineer to the Tees Conservancy Commissioners, and is now owned by the Tees and Hartlepool Port Authority.

Whitby, 2 miles (3 km) south-east of Whitby, NZ 928102. Two towers were built on Ling Hill by James Walker in 1858; the taller tower was removed in 1890 when a more powerful light was installed in the 43 feet (13 metres) high tower, which stands between the keepers' houses.

The West Pier lighthouse at Whitby, North Yorkshire, was erected in 1831 by Francis Pickernell, Whitby Harbour Engineer. The 70 feet (21 metres) high fluted stone column is topped by an octagonal lantern. The pier itself was built by Jonathan Pickernell in the early nineteenth century.

IRELAND

ANTRIM

Maidens, on Maidens Rocks (Hulin Rocks) off Larne. Two lighthouses were built in 1828–9 by George Halpin senior. West Rock light abandoned 1903; east light (white with black band) automated 1977.

Rathlin Island, off north coast of Antrim. Three lighthouses: Rathlin East on Altacarry Head, designed by George Halpin senior, built in 1849–56 (probably by George Halpin junior); Rathlin West (1919); Rue Point (1921).

CLARE

Loophead, marks northern approach to River Shannon. First lighthouse (*c.*1670) was a low, stone building holding a fire-platform with a coal-burning brazier. Present lighthouse built 1854.

CORK

Fastnet, south-west of Clear Island. First light, built 1854 from cast iron, was found to tremble and, although strengthened, was replaced by a granite tower completed in 1904 to the design of William Douglass. The 177 feet (54 metres) high tower is the tallest rock lighthouse tower in the British Isles.

Old Head of Kinsale, headland south of Kinsale. Built 1850–3 by George Halpin junior; 98 feet (30 metres) high tower originally white with red bands, changed to black with two white bands 1930.

Youghal. First light built at St Anne's Convent in 1190 by Maurice Fitzgerald. Second light built on same site 1852.

DONEGAL

Inishtrahull, island north-east of Malin Head. Original tower built 1812–13 (demolished 1959); it was the first lighthouse to be erected by George Halpin senior as Engineer to the Ballast Board. Present light is a reinforced concrete 76 feet (23 metres) high tower, built 1957–8.

Rinrawros Point, Aran Island. First lit 1798. (See pages 10, 25.)

Tory Island, off north-west coast of Donegal. Lighthouse (1832) originally used oil lamps; these were replaced 1885–7 by a gas apparatus invented by the lighting engineer John Wigham of Dublin.

DOWN

Mew Island, southern approach to Belfast Lough. Lighthouse (1884) is a barely tapering 121 feet (37 metres) high black tower, with a broad white band since 1954.

DUBLIN

Baily, Howth Head, north of Dublin Bay. Cottage-style lighthouse including a short, square stone tower was built on Howth Head *c.*1667. This coal-burning beacon was replaced in 1790 by a circular tower bearing oil lamps, but this was often obscured by fog and was itself replaced in 1813–14 with a lighthouse built by George Halpin senior at a low level on the headland.

KERRY

Inishtearaght, inhospitable islet west of Great Blasket Island. Most westerly lighthouse in Ireland, lit 1870. Designed by Charles Cotton, Engineer to the Port of Dublin 1863–7, consultant to the Commissioners of Irish Lights 1867–8.

LOUTH

Haulbowline Rock, rocky shoal at the mouth of Carlingford Lough. Lighthouse (1823–4) is an elegant, tapering stone tower rising 111 feet (34 metres) above sea level; built for the Ballast Board by George Halpin senior.

SLIGO
Blackrock, Sligo Bay. Solid stone beacon (1819) converted to lighthouse by George Halpin senior in 1833–5; white with single black band.

WEXFORD
Hook Head, eastern approach to Waterford Harbour. Oldest lighthouse still in use in the British Isles. (See page 5.)
Tuskar Rock, islet east of Carnsore Point. Granite tower (1811–15) was the first rock light to be built by George Halpin senior; it stands 112 feet (34 metres) high.

ISLE OF MAN
Calf of Man, on west coast of Calf of Man, an island at the south-west tip of the Isle of Man, SC 149657. Two lighthouses, both stone towers, were built in 1818 by Robert Stevenson; the galleries have cast-iron railings. The lights, which still stand, were discontinued in 1875

Left: *A lighthouse, in shape a squat round tower, was erected on Douglas Head, Isle of Man, in 1832–3 by the Isle of Man Harbour Commissioners; it was the successor to a daymark tower. Its eight-reflector light was visible for 15 miles (24 km). The Northern Lighthouse Board took over the lighthouse in 1857 and it was rebuilt in 1892 by the Board's engineers David Alan Stevenson and Charles Stevenson. The 66 feet (20 metres) high white tower, which rapidly became a tourist attraction, stands high on the headland above Douglas harbour and shows a white flashing light.*

Right: *The white tower of Langness Point lighthouse is a well-known landmark for those flying into Ronaldsway airport on the Isle of Man. Sited on the south-eastern tip of the island, the lighthouse was built in 1880 and designed by David and Thomas Stevenson. There are seventy-seven steps to the top of the 62 feet (19 metres) high tower, which shows a white light flashing twice every 30 seconds.*

Left: *The 76 feet (23 metres) high white tower of Maughold Head lighthouse on the Isle of Man was built in 1911–14. Construction, under the supervision of David Alan Stevenson, was difficult as the lighthouse was sited almost halfway up a sheer 200 feet (61 metres) high cliff face. The keepers' cottages (now private houses) on the cliff top are connected to the lighthouse below by 128 steps.*

Above left: *Point of Ayre lighthouse, Isle of Man, cost around £3500 to build in 1815–18 and was originally equipped with Argand lamps having reflectors 2 feet (0.6 metres) in diameter. Accommodation was provided for a keeper, an assistant and their families; a rough track led to the nearest village and it was 5 miles (8 km) down the coast to the town of Ramsey. Although the former keepers' accommodation is now holiday flats, the lighthouse retains its air of remoteness.*

Above right: *The Point of Ayre, Isle of Man, secondary light and foghorn, both built in 1890 to counter difficulties caused by gravel accretion extending the foreshore north-east of the light tower. The minor light, with its two balconies (one halfway up the polygonal tower), was moved even further seaward in 1951 and now stands on a gravel bank. The foghorn could be heard on the Mull of Galloway, 26 miles (42 km) away.*

when nearby Chicken Rock lighthouse was lit, but a new lighthouse was built in 1966–8. Its octagonal tower was constructed from reconstituted granite blocks.

Chicken Rock, off the south-west tip of the island, SC 143639. The lighthouse was built in 1869–75 by David and Thomas Stevenson. Its tapered granite tower is 144 feet (44 metres) high; the light has a range of 13 miles (21 km) and was automated in 1962. (See page 35.)

Douglas Head, south of Douglas, SC 390747. Rebuilt 1892.

Langness Point, south of Ronaldsway, SC 283653. Built 1880. (See page 49.)

Maughold Head, east of Ramsey, SC 498914. Built 1911–14. (See page 49.)

Point of Ayre, northern tip of Isle of Man, NX 467051. Built 1815–18.

SCOTLAND
ABERDEEN
Girdleness, south of Aberdeen, NJ 972054. Built by Robert Stevenson 1833. White round tower with gallery about one-third of its height above ground. Originally, this was glazed and showed a second light provided by thirteen lamps and reflectors; new lantern fitted on the main light in 1847. The double light was discontinued in 1890, when the main light was changed from a fixed to a flashing light.

ABERDEENSHIRE
Buchan Ness, Boddam, south of Peterhead, NK 137423. Built by Robert Stevenson 1827; new dioptric apparatus fitted in an enlarged lantern in 1910. White 115 feet (35 metres) high tower with red bands.

The Mull of Kintyre lighthouse was built in 1786–8 on remote cliffs 240 feet (73 metres) above the sea near the southern tip of Kintyre. The squat yellow tower, designed by the architect Robert Kay of Edinburgh, was the second lighthouse to be built by the Commissioners of Northern Lighthouses.

Kinnaird Head, Fraserburgh, NJ 998675. Small white tower built within the walls of a castellated sixteenth-century tower house by Thomas Smith in 1787; was the first lighthouse to be built by the Commissioners of Northern Lighthouses.

Rattray Head, between Fraserburgh and Peterhead, NK 111578. Unusual lighthouse built 1892–5 by David Alan Stevenson. Has granite drum base on which is set, asymmetrically, a slender tower of enamelled white brick; overall height 112 feet (34 metres).

ANGUS

Bell Rock, 11 miles (18 km) south-east of Arbroath, NO 762270. Built by Robert Stevenson 1807–10, making use of horizontal dovetailing of the masonry; first lit 1811. Base faced in Aberdeen granite, with sandstone from Dundee and Edinburgh used for remainder of tower; 2835 stones were used, all shipped from Arbroath, the shore base. The 100 feet (31 metres) high white tower is the oldest extant rock light in Britain. Two warning bells, linked to a clockwork mechanism, rang every thirty seconds in foggy or stormy weather.

ARGYLL AND BUTE

Dubh Artach, reef 16 miles (25 km) north-west of Colonsay, NM 122030. Built by David and Thomas Stevenson in 1868–72. Grey granite tower with broad red band; height 125 feet (38 metres). Storms during the construction of the lighthouse were so fierce that landings on the reef could be made on only 243 days in five working seasons.

McArthur's Head, east coast of Islay, NR 462597. Short white tower built 1861; shows red and white light.

Mull of Kintyre, southern tip of Kintyre, NR 587085. Built 1788.

Rinns of Islay, on Orsay, off western tip of Islay,

A milestone on the road leading down to the Mull of Kintyre lighthouse. Its construction entailed landing men and materials at Carskiey, a small inlet 5 miles (8 km) to the east, then transporting everything by horse on the difficult day-long journey across the peninsula. The builder was Peter Stuart of Campbeltown.

NR 164515. White tower built by Robert Stevenson 1825; its light was alternately stationary and revolving.

Ruvaal, northern tip of Islay, NR 426794. White 112 feet (34 metres) high tower built 1859. Optic supplied by Chance Brothers of Birmingham.

Sanda, Ship Rock, off Sanda Island, south of Kintyre, NR 725038. Built 1850. The lightkeeper's cottages at the base of the rock are connected to the lighthouse via stairs within two castellated stone towers, which step up the rock to the short light tower on its summit.

Skerryvore, reef off Tiree, NL 840263. Tapering, grey granite 158 feet (48 metres) high tower built by Alan Stevenson 1838–44; tallest lighthouse in Scotland.

DUMFRIES AND GALLOWAY

Corsewall, northern end of The Rhins, NW 981727. Built 1815–16 by Robert Stevenson, with two-storey flat-roofed keepers' houses; 86 feet (26 metres) high white-painted whinstone tower with balcony at first-floor level. Copper-domed lantern; light flashes red and white.

Mull of Galloway, southern tip of The Rhins, NX 157304. Built 1828–30 by Robert Stevenson; contractors were Brebner and Scott of Edinburgh. The round, white-painted rubblestone tower is 60 feet (18 metres) high; semicircular wall of stones at base.

EAST LOTHIAN

Barns Ness, east of Dunbar, NT 723773. Barely tapered 121 feet (37 metres) high circular stone tower built 1899–1901 by David Alan Stevenson. The first sealed beam lamps in a British lighthouse were installed here in April 1966.

Bass Rock, island east of North Berwick, NT 603874. Built 1902–3 by David Alan Stevenson on the site of a ruined castle.

FIFE

Inchkeith, islet in Firth of Forth, NT 293829. Built 1804 by Thomas Smith and Robert Stevenson. Stands on the site of a sixteenth-century fort; circular tower rises from castellated, two-storey base building, and whole structure resembles a miniature stone fortress. On 1st October 1835, the first Fresnel dioptric lens system to be installed in a British lighthouse began working at Inchkeith.

Isle of May, in Firth of Forth, NT 654994. Square, rubble-built tower with brazier built 1636; about 39 feet (12 metres) high. Replaced 1815–16 by lighthouse designed by Robert Stevenson in form of tiny picturesque castle. Lantern dates from 1924, keepers' house 1885. The low light, a round, white tower (now disused) and the adjacent cottages built 1844.

Holborn Head lighthouse stands on the cliffside just north of Thurso, commanding the entrance to Thurso Bay. The squat, white tower springs from the double-pile block of keepers' cottages below. It was built in 1860–2 by David and Thomas Stevenson.

HIGHLAND

Ardnamurchan, Point of Ardnamurchan, NM 416676. Built 1849. (See page 35.)

Cape Wrath, most north-westerly point of Scottish mainland, NC 259748. White tower built 1828 by Robert Stevenson; contractor John Gibb of Aberdeen. Originally had revolving light showing red and white.

Chanonry, Chanonry Point, east of Fortrose, NH 750557. Built by Alan Stevenson in 1846; white tower on semicircular base, octagonal lantern. Egyptian detail on keepers' accommodation. Automated 1984.

Cromarty, Cromarty, north end of Black Isle, overlooking entrance to Cromarty Firth, NH 787678. Built by Alan Stevenson in 1846; white tower on semicircular base, octagonal lantern. Egyptian detail on keepers' accommodation. Automated 1985; now base of the University of Aberdeen Marine Research Station.

Duncansby Head, north-east tip of Scottish mainland, ND 405734. Tapering, short square tower built 1924 by David Alan Stevenson; separate large foghorn.

Dunnet Head, east of Thurso, most northerly point of mainland Britain, ND 203768. Short, white stone tower, circular with semicircular offices at base, built by Robert Stevenson 1830–3 on cliff-top. A new optic was installed in 1852. (See page 9.)

Holborn Head, at entrance to Thurso Bay, ND 107707. Built 1860–2.

Neist Point, Skye, NG 126472. Built 1909.

Noss Head, north of Wick, ND 388551. White stone tower built in 1849 by Alan Stevenson. Keepers' cottages with Egyptian detail.

Rubha Reidh, west of Ullapool, NG 740918. Built 1912.

Stoer Head, north of Lochinver, NC 003330. Short, round white tower built 1870 by David and Thomas Stevenson; connected to two-storey keepers' accommodation.

Strathy Point, west of Thurso, NC 828697. Low white tower built 1958; first Scottish lighthouse to be built as an all-electric station. The lantern tower is square and built of concrete.

Tarbat Ness, north-eastern tip of Easter Ross, NH 947876. Stone tower 135 feet (41 metres) high built 1830 by Robert Stevenson; two red bands painted on white tower in 1915.

Above: *Neist Point lighthouse was built in 1909 on the most westerly point of Skye by David Alan Stevenson, who built a total of twenty-five lighthouses for the Northern Lighthouse Board (including three designed in collaboration with Thomas Stevenson).*

Right: *Rubha Reidh lighthouse was built on the headland of the same name, west of Ullapool, in 1912 by David Alan Stevenson and Charles Stevenson; the double-galleried lighthouse was automated in 1986.*

Hoy Low, which stands at the north-west tip of Graemsay, was one of a pair of lights built by Alan Stevenson in 1851 to guide ships into Hoy Sound from the west. The white-painted granite tower is 39 feet (12 metres) high; an adjacent Second World War observation tower is nearly as tall as the lighthouse.

MORAY
Covesea Skerries, west of Lossiemouth, NJ 204714. Thin white tower designed by Alan Stevenson in 1844–6.

NORTH AYRSHIRE
Holy Island, off east coast of Arran. First lighthouse was the inner or south-west light, built near the southern tip of the island, overlooking Lamlash Bay, in 1877 by David and Thomas Stevenson; it showed a fixed green light. This small white tower, with circular cross-section, still stands at NS 063287. The outer or south-east light at Pillar Rock, NS 068292, overlooking the Firth of Clyde, was built in 1905 by David Alan Stevenson.

Pladda, off southern tip of Arran, NS 028190. Built 1790. (See page 12.)

ORKNEY
Auskerry, island 3 miles (5 km) south of Stronsay, HY 673155. Tapered white 112 feet (34 metres) high tower built in brick by David and Thomas Stevenson in 1865–7.

Cantick Head, South Walls, ND 347894. Tapered white-painted brick tower built by David and Thomas Stevenson 1856–8; corbelled walkway below octagonal lantern.

Hoy High, north-east tip of Graemsay, HY 267063; *Hoy Low*, north-west tip of Graemsay, HY 247067. Both granite towers were built by Alan Stevenson in 1851. The elegant tower of Hoy High stands 108 feet (33 metres) high. A spiral stair leads up to the light-room, with its decorative, circular brass ventilators; above is the lantern, where lion heads adorn the glazing bars.

Kirkwall (Orkney Mainland) harbour light was built in 1880–5; its tapering cast-iron column rises from a square base. The pentagonal lantern platform is supported by corbels in the shape of seamen's heads.

Noup Head lighthouse on the north-western tip of Westray in the Orkney Islands was built by David Alan Stevenson in 1898. The brick-built, white-painted tower stands near cliffs that harbour a puffin colony.

North Ronaldsay, northern tip of North Ronaldsay, HY 784560. A 70 feet (21 metres) high beacon was put up in 1786–9; it has been disused since 1809. The second light, a red brick tower, was built in 1851–4 by Alan and David Stevenson. At 139 feet (42 metres), it is the tallest land-based lighthouse in Britain. The tower was painted with two white bands in 1889.

Pentland Skerries, on Muckle Skerry, north-east of Duncansby Head, ND 465785. Two towers were built by Thomas Smith and Robert Stevenson in 1794, standing 80 feet (24 metres) and 60 feet (18 metres) high, and 60 feet (18 metres) apart. The towers were rebuilt and raised during the 1820s, but the double light system was discontinued in 1895. A fog signal was placed on the low light tower in 1905, leaving the high light on its white tower, which stands 118 feet (36 metres) high.

Start Point, Sanday, HY 787435. Built 1869–70.

Sule Skerry, island 37 miles (60 km) west of Orkney, HX 620250. White 89 feet (27 metres) high tower built 1892–5 by David Alan Stevenson. The lantern, at 16 feet (5 metres) in diameter, was the largest in any lighthouse at the time.

Start Point lighthouse, Sanday. After the lighting of North Ronaldsay beacon (1789) to the north of Start Point, ships began to pass dangerously close to Sanday, which was equipped with its own daymark in 1802. A light was fitted in 1806, and the flat-roofed keepers' houses still stand alongside the striking 1870 tower; the old tower has been demolished.

The low, white tower of St Abbs Head lighthouse on its headland (above smugglers' caves) north of Eyemouth; it was built in 1862 by David and Thomas Stevenson. The light, which was converted to electricity in 1968, lies below the level of the keepers' cottages. The first siren fog signal in Scotland was installed at St Abbs in 1876.

SCOTTISH BORDERS
St Abbs Head, north of Eyemouth, NT 915694. Built 1862.

SHETLAND
Esha Ness, north-west of Shetland mainland, HU 206785. Tapering, square tower built by David Alan Stevenson 1925–9; constructed from concrete rather than the unsuitable local stone.

Muckle Flugga, island north of Unst, HP 607197. The most northerly lighthouse in the British Isles. Temporary lighthouse erected 1854; permanent light, a 64 feet (20 metres) high brick tower, built 1855–8 by David and Thomas Stevenson. The resident engineer was Alan Brebner, later a partner in the Stevenson family firm.

Out Skerries, on Bound Skerry, HU 702719. Tall white tower built by David and Thomas Stevenson in 1854.

Sumburgh Head, southern tip of Shetland mainland, HU 407079. Built by Robert Stevenson in 1821, with walls of double thickness to combat the damp conditions.

SOUTH AYRSHIRE
Ailsa Craig, island off Girvan, NX 026997. Built by Thomas and David Alan Stevenson in 1886. The lighthouse stands on a gravel spit on the east of the island, with two separate fog signals at the northern and southern points. The fog signals were operated by compressed air piped round the rock from the lighthouse.

Turnberry, north of Turnberry, NS 196074. White tower 79 feet (24 metres) high with yellow lantern, built 1873 by David and Thomas Stevenson; beside golf course.

WESTERN ISLES
Barra Head, on Berneray, NL 549804. White stone tower built 1833 by Robert Stevenson.

Butt of Lewis, northern tip of Isle of Lewis, NB 520666. Tapering, red-brick 121 feet (37 metres) high tower built by David and Thomas Stevenson in 1859–62.

Eilean Glas, on Scalpay, NG 247947. Built by Thomas Smith in 1788–9. The red and white banded 98 feet (30 metres) high tower was rebuilt during the 1820s; changed from fixed to flashing light in 1907.

Flannan Islands, on Eilean Mor, NA 727469. White tower built in 1896–9 by David Alan Stevenson. The last of the great nineteenth-century Scottish lighthouses. Infamous for the mysterious disappearance of all three lightkeepers on 15th December 1900; they were probably washed away by high seas.

Tiumpan Head, Eye Peninsula, Isle of Lewis, NB 574377. Built in 1900 by David Alan Stevenson; round, white tower 69 feet (21 metres) high.

The lightship 'Helwick LV14' was last stationed off the Gower Peninsula, where it marked the Helwick Swatch, a dangerous sandbank; its light could be seen at a distance of 25 miles (40 km). It had a crew of eleven, seven of whom were on board at any one time. At the end of its working life the 137 feet (42 metres) long vessel was restored to become a floating Christian centre and moored on the redeveloped Cardiff Bay waterfront; it is known as the 'Goleulong 2000' lightship and is open to the public.

Ushenish, east coast of South Uist, NF 874351. White tower built in 1857 by David and Thomas Stevenson.

WALES
CARDIFF
Flatholm, island of Flatholm in the Bristol Channel, ST 222647. The lighthouse, a circular stone tower, was built in 1737; the open platform was replaced by an enclosed lantern in 1820. An iron gallery and larger lantern were added in 1867, when the height of the tower was 95 feet (29 metres).

CONWY
Great Ormes Head, west of Llandudno, SH 756845. Castellated stone structure built on the cliff top by the Mersey Docks and Harbour Board in 1862; the lantern or lens room sits at ground level in front of the main building. Taken over by Trinity House in 1973, but discontinued in 1985 and converted to a private house.

GWYNEDD
Bardsey, on Bardsey Island, off Lleyn Peninsula, SH 111206. Built 1821. (See pages 13, 26.)
St Tudwal's, on St Tudwal's West Island, south-east of Lleyn Peninsula, SH 334252. A 35 feet (11 metres) high stone tower built in 1877 shows red and white lights.

The village of Portmeirion was designed by the architect Clough Williams-Ellis and opened in 1926. This folly lighthouse, which marks Portmeirion's southernmost point, was designed by Williams-Ellis and built in 1954 (renovated 1996). It is made of sheet metal and crowned by an upturned pigswill boiler with an ornate finial. It stands in woodlands a short walk along the coastal path from the village.

Skokholm lighthouse on Skokholm Island, west of Milford Haven in Pembrokeshire, was built in 1915. Its 58 feet (18 metres) high octagonal white tower rises from the flat-roofed two-storey keepers' cottages. The lighthouse was automated in 1983 and the little island, with its sheer cliffs, is now a bird sanctuary.

ISLE OF ANGLESEY

Point Lynas, north coast of Anglesey, SH 479936. Light established 1779; current lighthouse built by Jesse Hartley for the Mersey Docks and Harbour Board in 1835. Taken over by Trinity House 1973. Low, white-painted castellated structure with lens room attached to building at ground level; shows white light.

Skerries, off north-west coast of Anglesey, SH 268948. Lighthouse first lit 1717, rebuilt *c*.1759, sold to Trinity House in 1841. It was the last privately owned lighthouse in the British Isles to be bought by Trinity House, for whom it was lavishly restored by James Walker around 1848. The early-eighteenth-century crow-stepped cottage is the oldest separate keepers' accommodation in Britain.

South Stack, small island west of Holyhead, SH 202823. Tapered, round 92 feet (28 metres) high tower built 1809 by Joseph Nelson; its engineer was Daniel Asher Alexander. The white tower, built from stone quarried on the site, was Nelson's first lighthouse and has hardly been altered. Access to the island is via 380 steps down to a slender aluminium bridge dating from 1964, when it replaced the suspension bridge of 1828.

Trwyn Du, off eastern tip of Anglesey, SH 644815. Built 1837–8; the black and white tower was the first Trinity House light to be converted to automatic working, in 1922. (See page 14.)

NEWPORT

West Usk, ST 311829. The former lighthouse stands on reclaimed land (still an island when the lighthouse was built) on the west bank of the River Usk at its meeting with the Severn estuary. A brick tower lit in 1821, it was the first of twenty-nine lighthouses designed by James Walker for Trinity House. Base of tower now encased by drum-shaped white-painted dwellings, added *c*.1867; lantern removed 1922, now replaced by replica.

PEMBROKESHIRE

Caldey Island, off Tenby, SS 143959. Round, limestone tower, 52 feet (16 metres) high, built by Joseph Nelson 1829. Lantern fitted mid nineteenth century.

St Ann's Head, west of Milford Haven, SM 806028. First lighthouse built 1660s, but light discontinued. A further tower built 1714, and both were lit. The 65 feet (20 metres) high rear light was in use until 1909 and still stands. The front light was rebuilt 1841, and is still in use;

it is a 43 feet (13 metres) high octagonal tower showing red and white lights.

Skokholm, on Skokholm Island, SM 729046. Built 1915.

Smalls, off St Brides Bay, SM 467089. The reef is the most westerly point in Wales, lying 21 miles (34 km) off St David's Head. First lighthouse, a piled structure of wood designed by Henry Whiteside, built 1776; infamous for incident shortly before 1801 in which one of the two keepers died and the other, fearing he might be suspected of murder, put the body in a box and lashed it to the lantern rail to await the relief boat. Second lighthouse, granite tower 135 feet (41 metres) high, erected under supervision of James and Nicholas Douglass to design by James Walker (based on Smeaton's Eddystone tower) in 1858–61. One of the first lighthouses (with Wolf Rock) to incorporate water closets for the keepers. Tower painted red and white until 1997, then grit-blasted back to natural granite.

South Bishop, islet west of Ramsey Island, SM 651226. The 37 feet (11 metres) high tower was built 1839 by James Walker. Gently tapering white, circular tower with iron railings around lantern platform; the iron lantern is largely original.

Strumble Head, west of Fishguard, SM 892413. A 55 feet (17 metres) high white tower built 1908. Stands on a small island reached by an iron bridge from the mainland.

SWANSEA

Mumbles, island just off Swansea, accessible from mainland on foot at low tide, SS 635873. Built by William Jernegan in 1793–4; two-tier white tower consists of two octagons, one inside the other, with a stair occupying the internal space. It carried upper and lower fire platforms; converted to a single, oil-lit lantern in 1798, and new lantern fitted around 1860.

VALE OF GLAMORGAN

Nash Point, Bristol Channel, on coast 7 miles (11 km) south of Bridgend, SS 921680. High and low lights (both white-painted stone towers) were built by Joseph Nelson in 1832. The low (west) light, 67 feet (20 metres) in height, was discontinued *c.*1900 but still stands beside the original 1832 keepers' cottage, which has four rooms surrounding a central chimney rising above a pyramidal roof. The high (east) light is 122 feet (37 metres) in height; new lantern fitted 1867, automated 1998.

Far left: *A beacon was lit on the watch-tower at Calais, on the northern coast of France, from 1818, but the present 174 feet (53 metres) high lighthouse dates from 1848. The octagonal tower, which stands in the centre of Calais, has a circular interior with 271 steps leading to the lantern. The light, which has been electric-powered since 1883, gives four flashes every fifteen seconds.*

Left: *The lighthouse at Cap Gris-Nez, on the northern coast of France about 15 miles (24 km) south-west of Calais, has a tower 102 feet (31 metres) in height.*

LIGHTHOUSES OF GREAT BRITAIN AND IRELAND

Shetland
Muckle Flugga
Esha Ness
Out Skerries
Bressay
Sumburgh Head

North Ronaldsay
Noup Head
Fair Isle North
Fair Isle South
Start Point
Orkney
Kirkwall
Auskerry
Sule Skerry
Hoy High
Copinsay
Cantick Head
Stroma
Cape Wrath
Dunnet Head
Pentland Skerries
Strathy
Duncansby Head
Butt of Lewis
Point
Holborn
Head
Noss Head
Flannan
Islands
Stoer
Head
Tiumpan
Head
Rubha Reidh
Tarbat
Ness
Kinnaird
Head
Eilean
Glas
Cromarty
Rattray Head
North
Rona
Covesea
Buchan Ness
Neist
Point
Chanonry
Skerries
Ushenish
Girdleness
Hyskeir
Tod Head
Barra Head
Ardnamurchan
SCOTLAND
Scurdie Ness
Corran
Skerryvore
Lismore
Bell Rock
Fife Ness
Isle of May
Dubh Artach
Fidra
Bass Rock
Ruvaal
Inchkeith
Barns Ness
Rinns of Islay
McArthur's
St Abbs Head
Head
Inishtrahull
Davaar
Holy Island
Bamburgh
Longstone
Rathlin
Pladda
Farne
Tory Island
Island
Mull of Kintyre
Fanad
Inishowen
Turnberry
Coquet
Rinrawros Point
Head
Head
Sanda
Ailsa Craig
Blyth
St Mary's
Corsewall
North Shields
Souter
Rathlin O'Birne
Maidens
Killantringan
Heugh
Black Head
South Gare
Eagle
St John's
Mew Island
Mull of
Island
Point
NORTHERN
Galloway
St Bees
Whitby
Blackrock
IRELAND
Donaghadee
Point of Ayre
Blackrock
St John's
ISLE OF
Maughold Head
Flamborough
Point
MAN
Douglas Head
Haulbowline
Calf of
Langness Point
Walney
Withernsea
Rock
Man
Chicken Rock
Fleetwood
Spurn Head
Slyne
South Killingholme
Head
Point
Great
Baily
Lynas
Ormes
see Wirral
Eeragh Island
Straw Island
Skerries
Head
inset
Inisheer
South Stack
Trwyn
Cromer
Scattery
Du
Hunstanton
Island
Wicklow Head
Portmeirion
Happisburgh
Loophead
Bardsey
St Tudwal's
Lowestoft
ENGLAND
Inishtearaght
Tuskar
Southwold
Rock
WALES
Orfordness
Skelligs
Dunmore East
Strumble
Youghal
Hook Head
Head
Bull Rock
Ballycotton
South Bishop
St Ann's Head
West
North
Fastnet
Galley
Old Head
Smalls
Mumbles
Usk
Foreland
Head
of Kinsale
Skokholm
Caldey
Nash
Flatholm
South Foreland
Island
Point
Burnham
Dover
Lundy North
Dungeness
Lundy South
Lynmouth
Bull
Foreland
Belle Tout
Hartland Point
Point
Trevose Head
Hurst Point
Anvil Point
Beachy Head
Mount
Batten Point
Berry
Needles
St Catherine's
Godrevy
Head
Portland
Pendeen
Bill
Longships
St Anthonys
Start Point
Round Island
Tater
Eddystone
Bishop Rock
Du
Lizard
Wolf
Rock

WIRRAL
New Brighton
Bidston Hill
Leasowe
Hoylake

CHANNEL ISLANDS
Alderney
Quenard
Point
Casquets
Guernsey
Sark
Les Hanois
Point Robert
La Corbiere
Jersey

Further reading

Adcock, Joy. *Lighthouse Accommodation*. Adcock, 2008.
Ashley, Peter. *Guiding Lights*. Everyman Publishers, 2001.
Bathurst, Bella. *The Lighthouse Stevensons*. HarperCollins, 1999.
Boyle, Martin. *Beachy Head*. B & T Publications, 1999.
Hague, Douglas B., and Christie, Rosemary. *Lighthouses: Their Architecture, History and Archaeology*. Gomer Press, 1995.
Hart-Davis, Adam, and Troscianko, Emily. *Henry Winstanley and the Eddystone Lighthouse*. Sutton Publishing, 2002.
Hellowell, John. *A Tour of Manx Lighthouses*. Peter Williams Associates, 1998.
Hume, John R. *Harbour Lights in Scotland*. Scottish Vernacular Buildings Working Group, 1997.
Renton, Alan. *Lost Sounds*. Whittles Publishing, 2001.
Trethewey, Ken, and Guichard, Jean. *North Atlantic Lighthouses*. Flammarion, 2002.
Woodman, Richard, and Wilson, Jane. *The Lighthouses of Trinity House*. Thomas Reed, 2002.

Websites

Association of Lighthouse Keepers: www.alk.org.uk
Commissioners of Irish Lights: www.cil.ie
Lighthouse Society of Great Britain: www.lsgb.co.uk
Northern Lighthouse Board: www.nlb.org.uk
Trinity House: www.trinityhouse.co.uk

The lighthouse at Cap de Creus, on the Mediterranean coast at Spain's most easterly point. The wild and rocky headland has always been a hazard to shipping; five Roman galleys were wrecked in the cove immediately north of the lighthouse.

Places to visit

Lighthouses and other places with lighthouse-related material on permanent display are listed below. However, displays may be altered and readers are advised to telephone before visiting to check that relevant items are on show, as well as to find out the times of opening.

Anvil Point, Durlston Country Park, near Swanage. Telephone: 07818 268191.

Arbroath Museum, Signal Tower, Ladyloan, Arbroath, Angus DD11 1PU. Telephone: 01241 875598. The signal tower was the shore base for the Bell Rock lighthouse, and the museum includes displays on the construction and history of Bell Rock.

Ardnamurchan Lighthouse, Ardnamurchan Point, Kilchoan by Acharacle, Ardnamurchan, Argyll PH36 4LN. Telephone: 01972 510210. Website: www.ardnamurchanlighthouse.com Visitor centre.

Bressay Lighthouse, Shetland Amenity Trust, 22–24 North Road, Lerwick, Shetland ZE1 0NQ. Telephone: 01595 820368. Marine heritage centre.

Dover Castle, Dover, Kent CT16 1HU. Telephone: 01304 201628 or 211067. Website: www.english-heritage.org.uk Roman pharos in the grounds of Dover Castle.

Dungeness Old Lighthouse, Dungeness Road, Dungeness, Romney Marsh, Kent TN29 9NB. Telephone: 01797 321300. Website: www.dungenesslighthouse.com

Flamborough Head Lighthouse, Flamborough, East Yorkshire. Telephone: 01262 673769.

Gairloch Heritage Museum, Achtercairn, Gairloch, Ross-shire IV21 2BP. Telephone: 01445 712287.

Goleulong 2000 Lightship, Harbour Drive, Cardiff Bay CF10 4PA. Telephone: 029 2048 7609. Former Trinity House light-vessel, now Christian centre.

Grace Darling Museum, 1 Radcliffe Road, Bamburgh, Northumberland NE69 7AE. Telephone: 01668 214910. Website: www.rnli.org.uk/gracedarling Collection of Grace Darling memorabilia, including the coble used in the famous rescue.

Great Orme Museum, Llandudno LL30 2XG. Telephone: 01492 870447. Summit of Great Orme, optic from Great Orme's Head lighthouse.

Happisburgh Lighthouse, Happisburgh, Norfolk NR12 0PY. Telephone: 01692 650803. Website: www.happisburgh.org/lighthouse Happisburgh Lighthouse Trust took over the running of the lighthouse from Trinity House in 1990.

Hook Lighthouse, Hook Head, Fethard-on-Sea, County Wexford. Website: www.thehook-wexford.com

Hurst Castle, Hurst Spit, Keyhaven, Lymington, Hampshire SO41 0QU. Telephone: 01590 642344. Website: www.hurstcastle.co.uk On pebble spit south of Keyhaven, commanding entrance to the Solent; best approached by ferry from Keyhaven. English Heritage, telephone: 0870 333 1181.

Hynish Signal Tower, Tiree, Argyll. Former signal tower for Skerryvore lighthouse; open all year, key available on request.

Kilmore Quay Maritime Museum, Kilmore Quay, Wexford, Ireland. Telephone: 053 29655. The museum is sited on the *Guillemot*, the last of the Irish lightships (built in 1922), which is still fully fitted out.

Leasowe Lighthouse, Leasowe Common, Moreton, Wirral CH46 4TA. Telephone: 0151 678 5488. Website: www.leasowlighthouse.co.uk

Lizard Heritage Centre, Lizard Point, Lizard, Cornwall. Telephone: 01326 290202.

Long Hill Lighthouse, near Wicklow, County Wicklow, Ireland. Telephone: 00 353 1 662 8425. Octagonal stone lighthouse built 1781; can be hired from the Irish Landmark Trust, 25 Eustace Street, Temple Bar, Dublin 2 (telephone: 00 353 1 670 4733).

Longstone Lighthouse, Farne Islands, Northumberland. Telephone: 01665 721210 or 721819 (tickets and information). Access by boat from Seahouses.

Maritime Museum, The Green, Harbour Crescent, Harwich, Essex CO12 3NJ. Telephone: 01255 503429. Museum occupies the former Low Lighthouse.

Mizen Head Visitor Centre, Mizen Head, Goleen, West Cork. Websites: www.mizenhead.ie and www.mizenhead.net

Mull of Galloway Lighthouse, near Stranraer. Telephone: 01776 830682. Website: www.mull-of-galloway.co.uk

Museum of Scottish Lighthouses, Kinnaird Head, Stevenson Road, Fraserburgh, Aberdeenshire AB43 9DU. Telephone: 01346 511022. Website: www.lighthousemuseum.org.uk Extensive collection relating to Scottish lighthouses and the Northern Lighthouse Board.

Nash Point Lighthouse, Marcross, near Bridgend. Website: www.trinityhouse.co.uk

North Foreland Lighthouse, Broadstairs, Kent CT10 3NW. Telephone: 01843 861869.

Pendeen Lighthouse, Pendeen, Penzance, Cornwall TR19 7ED. Telephone: 01736 788418.

Portland Bill Lighthouse, Easton, Isle of Portland, Dorset DT5 2JT. Telephone: 01305 820495. Museum and visitor centre at the lighthouse.

Quénard Point Lighthouse, Alderney. Telephone: 01481 822522 or 824309.

St Catherine's Lighthouse, Niton, Isle of Wight. Telephone: 01983 855069. Website: www.trinityhouse.co.uk

St Catherine's Oratory, Niton, Ventnor, Isle of Wight. Medieval lighthouse in the care of English Heritage (property managed by the National Trust). External viewing only, any reasonable time.

St Mary's Lighthouse, Whitley Bay, Northumberland NE26 4RS. Telephone: 0191 200 8650/8652. Website: www.friendsofstmaryisland.co.uk The lighthouse is accessible by a short causeway from the mainland at low tide. Good views from the lantern.

Scottish Fisheries Museum, St Ayles, Harbourhead, Anstruther, Fife KY10 3AB. Telephone: 01333 310628. Website: www.scotfishmuseum.org Display includes the light-vessel *North Carr*, previously moored off Fife Ness.

Smeaton's Tower, The Hoe, Plymouth, Devon PL1 2NZ. Website: www.plymouth.gov.uk/museumsmeatonstower. The upper part of Smeaton's Eddystone lighthouse was erected on the Hoe after it was replaced by the fourth Eddystone light in 1882. There are good views from the lantern.

Souter Lighthouse, Coast Road, Whitburn, Sunderland SR6 7NH. Telephone: 0191 529 3161. Website: www.nationaltrust.org.uk In the care of the National Trust; visitors may see the tower, engine room, fog-signal station and keeper's cottage.

South Foreland Lighthouse, St Margaret's at Cliffe, Dover. Telephone: 01304 852463. Website: www.nationaltrust.org.uk Visitors may climb the tower, from which there are views to France.

South Stack Lighthouse, Holyhead, Anglesey, North Wales LL65 1YH. Telephone: 01407 763207. The lighthouse is on a small island connected to the mainland cliffs by 400 steps.

Southwold Lighthouse, Southwold, Suffolk. Telephone: 01502 722576.

Spurn Lightship, Hull Marina, Hull HU1 2BX. Telephone: 01482 593902. Website: www.hullcc.gov.uk Visitors may see the light mechanism, master's cabin and crew's quarters.

Start Point Lighthouse, Stokenham, Devon. Telephone: 01803 770606.

Trinity Buoy Wharf, 64 Orchard Place, London E14 0JW. Telephone: 020 7515 7153. Website: www.trinitybuoywharf.com London's only lighthouse; good riverside views.

Trinity House, Broad Chare, Newcastle upon Tyne NE1 3DQ. Telephone: 0191 232 8226. Website: www.trinityhousenewcastle.org.uk Guided tours only, by prior arrangement. Buildings include the chapel (1505) and banqueting hall (1721); the museum display includes the old light apparatus (a combination of eight reflectors) from the *Shipwash* light-vessel, sited off Orfordness, Suffolk.

Wick Heritage Museum, 18-27 Bank Row, Wick KW1 5EY. Telephone: 01955 605393. Website: www.wickheritage.org Displays optical and mechanical works from Noss Head lighthouse.

Withernsea Lighthouse Museum, The Lighthouse, Hull Road, Withernsea, East Yorkshire HU19 2DY. Telephone: 01964 614834. Website: www.withernsealighthouse.co.uk The lighthouse was closed in 1976 and is now a museum; good views from the tower, a climb of 144 steps

Index of lighthouses

Ailsa Craig 35, 56
Anvil Point 41
Aranmore 10, 25, 48
Ardnamurchan 35, 53, 62
Auskerry 54
Baily 48
Bamburgh 44
Bardsey 13, 26, 57
Barns Ness 52
Barra Head 56
Bass Rock 52
Beachy Head 46
Bell Rock 10, 18-19, 20, 22, 51, 62
Belle Tout 46
Berry Head 40
Bidston 22, 38
Bishop Rock 9, 22, 39
Blackrock 49
Blyth 45
Bow Creek 3, 43, 63
Bressay 62
Bridport 26
Buchan Ness 50
Bull Point 40
Burnham 45
Butt of Lewis 56
Calais 59
Caldey Island 58
Calf of Man 35, 49
Cantick Head 54
Cap de Creus 61
Cap Gris-Nez 59
Cape Wrath 53
Casquets 14, 38
Chanonry 53
Chicken Rock 35, 50
Coquet 20, 44
Cordouan 28
Corsewall 52
Corton 8
Covesea Skerries 54
Cromarty 53
Cromer 8, 43
Davaar 14
Douglas Head 49, 50
Dover 4, 62
Dovercourt 19, 20, 41
Dubh Artach 10, 51
Duncansby Head 53
Dungeness 31, 32, 42, 62
Dunnet Head 9, 53
East Goodwin LV 23
Eddystone 9, 10, 12-16, 23-4, 26, 32, 36,
    37, 39, 40, 59, 63
Eilean Glas 56
Esha Ness 56
Farne 8, 44
Fastnet 21, 48
Flamborough 7, 8, 47, 62
Flannan Islands 37, 56
Flatholm 14, 57
Fleetwood 43
Girdleness 50
Godrevy 12, 39
Great Ormes Head 57

Groyne (South Shields) 37
Happisburgh 44, 62
Hartland Point 41
Harwich High 8, 19, 41
Harwich Low 8, 19, 41, 62
Haulbowline Rock 48
Helwick LV 57
Heugh 41
Holborn Head 52, 53
Holy Island 54
Hook Head 5, 49
Hoy High 54
Hoy Low 54
Hoylake 38
Hunstanton 44
Hurst Point 41, 42
Inchkeith 52
Inishtearaght 48
Inishtrahull 48
Isle of May 52
Killingholme High 43
Killingholme North Low 43
Killingholme South Low 43
Kinnaird Head 10, 51
Kirkwall 54
Kish Bank LV 33
La Corbière 24, 38
Langness Point 49, 50
Lawe Top 5
Leasowe 17, 38, 62
Les Hanois 22-3, 38
Lismore 15
Lizard 8, 39, 62
Long Hill 62
Longships 39
Longstone 11, 45, 62
Loophead 48
Lowestoft 7, 46
Lundy North 40, 41
Lundy Old 2, 40, 41
Lundy South 41
Lynmouth Foreland 41
Maidens 48
Maplin Sands 20-1
Maughold Head 49, 50
McArthur's Head 51
Mew Island 48
Mount Batten Point 27
Muckle Flugga 10, 56
Mull of Galloway 52, 62
Mull of Kintyre 51
Mumbles 59
Nash Point 59
Needles 42
Neist Point 53
New Brighton 38
Nore Bank 32
North Foreland 6, 7, 42, 63
North Ronaldsay 55
North Shields 7, 26, 45
Noss Head 53
Noup Head 55
Old Head of Kinsale 48
Orfordness 7, 46
Out Skerries 56

Pendeen 22, 39, 63
Pentland Skerries 55
Perch Rock 38
Pladda 12, 54
Point Lynas 58
Point of Ayre 50
Point Robert 38
Portland Bill 41, 63
Portmeirion 57
Quénard Point 38, 63
Rathlin Island 48
Rattray Head 51
Rinns of Islay 51
Rinrawros Point 10, 25, 48
Round Island 39
Royal Sovereign LV 33
Rubha Reidh 53
Ruvaal 52
St Abbs Head 56
St Agnes 8, 27
St Ann's Head 58
St Anthony's 39
St Bees 26, 36, 39
St Catherine's (Isle of Wight) 5-6, 42, 63
St Catherine's Point (Cornwall) 25
St Mary's 22, 23, 30, 45, 63
St Michael's Mount 27
St Tudwal's 57
Sanda 52
Skerries 8, 14, 58
Skerryvore 19-20, 52, 62
Skokholm 58, 59
Smalls 17, 21, 34, 59
Souter 21, 29, 30, 33, 34, 35, 41, 63
South Bishop 59
South Foreland 7, 28, 31, 42, 63
South Gare 47
South Stack 58, 63
Southwold 46, 63
Spurn Head 9, 47
Spurn LV 33, 63
Start Point (Devon) 41, 63
Start Point (Orkney) 2, 55
Stoer Head 53
Strathy Point 53
Strumble Head 59
Sule Skerry 55
Sumburgh Head 56
Swansea 20
Tarbat Ness 53
Tater Du 39
Tiumpan Head 56
Tory Island 48
Trevose Head 39
Trwyn Du 14, 37, 58
Turnberry 56
Tuskar Rock 49
Ushenish 57
Walney 36, 39
West Usk 58
Whitby 47
Withernsea 1, 23, 30, 47, 63
Wolf Rock 21, 39, 59, 63
Youghal 48